INSIDE OUT

INSIDE OUT

Kimberly Daniels

Charisma
HOUSE
A STRANG COMPANY

Most STRANG COMMUNICATIONS/CHARISMA HOUSE/SILOAM/FRONTLINE/
EXCEL BOOKS/REALMS products are available at special quantity discounts for
bulk purchase for sales promotions, premiums, fund-raising, and educational
needs. For details, write Strang Communications/Charisma House/Siloam/
FrontLine/Excel Books/Realms, 600 Rinehart Road, Lake Mary, Florida
32746, or telephone (407) 333-0600.

INSIDE Out by Kimberly Daniels
Published by Charisma House
A Strang Company
600 Rinehart Road
Lake Mary, Florida 32746
www.charismahouse.com

Design Director: Bill Johnson
Cover Designer: Justin Evans
Author Photograph © Reggie Anderson Photography

Library of Congress Cataloging-in-Publication Data

Daniels, Kimberly.
  Inside out / Kim Daniels. -- 1st ed.
     p. cm.
  ISBN 978-1-59979-279-8
  1. Christian life. 2. Spiritual healing. 3. Spiritual warfare. I. Title.

BV4501.3.D36 2008
248.8'6--dc22

                                    2007052281

First Edition

08 09 10 11 12—987654321
Printed in the United States of America

CONTENTS

FOREWORD

SEEKING THE LORD concerning inner healing requires the unadulterated truth. People in general avoid pain and conflict, but transparency is imperative when it comes to being content and unbroken. As a person who has experienced immense rejection, I sought for years a healing I thought would never come. As a child and up until my young adult years, I believed I was the nobody that anybody didn't want. As a result of the rejection, I have struggled with sexual identity, being a people pleaser, and self-centeredness. At one point in my life I didn't even know who I was because I was so detached from what was inside. I lived life by the externals, which constantly changed; therefore, I didn't live.

No matter how things appeared on the outside, what was inside remained mixed and uncommitted. Just as the Pharisees of the Bible were called hypocrites, so was my perspective on life. I'll be the first to admit that faking it just won't make it happen in the Lord. Though years ago, my insides were "jacked up" while attending a church. I gave what I didn't have to be seen; I smoked "the herb" of heaven and walked around perpetrating the gospel: living a lie while representing the truth. All in all, I was a hypocrite in need of a healing. I share my past in hopes of bringing someone to the place where the truth will set him or her free enough to be healed.

It took years of cyclical mistakes and regrets before I found the truth as to who I was to God and myself. I came to know who I was by the

Spirit of God, not by the past dictates of tormenting memories. I realized that my testimony was only as great as my acceptance of God's forgiveness through His love for me. According to the ancient rabbis, it is said that the greatest worship of man is to fulfill the destiny of being "Tzelem and Demuth," image and likeness. It is to be the appearance and action of the Almighty, the Creator of all. Most miss this wonderful opportunity by busying themselves with "doing" instead of "being."

We can be our greatest enemies, and with time working against us using the past, we can risk forfeiture of God's gift—life. It is a dangerous combination when time passes without true healing from life's bumps and bruises. I know; I have lived through some. Every person struggles while God is ready to sincerely forgive through those struggles. I remember when I attended a Christian church during my early walk of accepting Yeshua as the Mashiach, I was told, "You're not Jewish anymore, but a Christian now." I grappled with this idea so much so that I denied my Hebraic roots. I recognize now that nothing grows without roots whether the tree is good or bad. Instead of drawing closer to God, things became distant and religious.

Today, being a Hebrew rabbi is not easy in a clearly anti-Semitic world. Being a Hebrew who believes in Yeshua can be even more difficult. Between the rejection from fellow Jews and the sometimes misinterpreted message within the Christian faith, it would be easy to give excuse of being "just downright ugly," but that kind of attitude would not please my heavenly Father. It is time for people to come as is—bent and broken. The need is great and the silent pleas deafening. Salvation is not liberating when the "issues" are real and the attacks grow greater. People are looking for answers to the questions of "Why me?" "Who am I?" and "Why am I here?" The global society is despondent, nonresponsive, and has been mentally mislabeled by the "experts" seeking to set trends. The world appears to be broken, but the Lord has His remnant in motion to set things in kingdom order.

I met apostles Ardell and Kimberly and the Spoken Word family during a time when clarity was my greatest cry before the Lord. What I have since then learned was the need for a greater healing of self. I believe it is only the Lord who builds a house, and my house (life), though founded by Him, needed builders who were able to see the Great Architect's plans, and this is what happened to me in the correct season. I have traveled throughout the world witnessing lives being restored in God. And because I believe true salvation is wholeness of spirit, soul, and body, this book, *Inside Out* by Apostle Kimberly Daniels, is a much-needed resource. I have experienced personal "awakening" and deliverance that have brought what I like to call the "real heal deal."

There is good and evil, choice and effect, as believers endeavor to stay in the will of God. As children of a God who forgives, we are given the grace to be and live as citizens of a holy kingdom. As you read this book, take a long and deep look at life. I encourage you to allow the Ruach HaKodesh (the Holy Spirit) to be the path and guide to the most important place within yourself—the truth. Truth is foundational to forgiveness and being healed to the utmost. Every relationship with the Lord has the expectation of one thing—to have an outward expression of an inward impression. When we are complete in Yeshua, praise is the ultimate evidence of coming into the Lord's presence because we get to experience the fullness of His joy in us. In Scripture we are instructed to praise the Lord.

> Let everything that has breath praise the LORD. Praise the LORD!
>
> —Psalm 150:6

Though this psalm is said across the world by many, the meaning is not given the full measure of appreciation. Regardless of how challenging life may appear, this psalm presents the invitation to instill: "With every breath we are to praise the Lord." Now breathe with adoration to the Lord and be whole.

—Rabbi Yisrael Ben Avraham
HaMishkan

INTRODUCTION

MOVING FORWARD . . .
INSIDE OUT!

I N GENESIS 2:7 Adam became a living soul. This word *soul* is
nephesh in Hebrew. It means:

+ Life
+ The seat of the appetite
+ The place of passion and emotion
+ The inner being of man
+ Activity of the mind and will
+ Character and being

God blew the breath (*ruwach*) of life into man, and he became a living
soul (*nephesh*). I am constantly amazed at how people attempt to live
without God in their lives. God made us living souls so that we would not
follow Him like zombies. He created a place of passion and emotion on
the inside of us so that we could love Him with all of our soul. Based on
this, Matthew 22:37 is actually saying that we should love the Lord with
all of the passion and emotion that God put on the inside of us.

Unfortunately the enemy has rerouted the appetites of men toward
passions that do not draw them to God. The result of this negative

activity in the mind and will of man is an existence rooted in outward prosperity with no inner wealth. In the New Testament, the Greek word *psuche* means "breath of life." It is related to the word *psyche*. It is said to be the seat of emotion, feeling, and desire. It is also defined as "the moral being designed for everlasting life…an essence [of man] which…is not dissolved by death."[1] This is the part of man that exists forever!

SOUL PROSPERITY IS THE KEY TO VICTORIOUS LIVING.

It is really easy to be distracted in life by focusing on things that are temporary. Abundant life is inevitable when we target the eternal. The outward appearance of things promotes that which is temporary, but inward essence promotes eternal things. Matthew 23:24–28 explains this best:

> Blind guides, who strain out a gnat and swallow a camel! Woe to you, scribes and Pharisees, hypocrites! For you cleanse the outside of the cup and dish, but inside they are full of extortion and self-indulgence. Blind Pharisee, first cleanse the inside of the cup and dish, that the outside of them may be clean also. Woe to you, scribes and Pharisees, hypocrites! For you are like white-washed tombs which indeed appear beautiful outwardly, but inside are full of dead men's bones and all uncleanness. Even so you also outwardly appear righteous to men, but inside you are full of hypocrisy and lawlessness.

The vision of this book is to release a message of wholeness from the inside out! Jesus warned us not to fear that which was able to kill the body, but to fear that which could kill the soul. This book identifies and deals with what can kill the body and gives edification to build up the soul. Soul prosperity is the key to victorious living.

Matthew 16:26 asks two questions:

1. What does it profit a man to gain the world and lose his soul?
2. What will a man exchange for his soul?

People who worship the outward appearance of the things of the world are subject to the fleshly lusts that war against the soul (1 Pet. 2:11). Hebrews 6:19 speaks of the anchor of the soul, or *agkura*. This is an inward safeguard that assures fidelity when infidelity knocks at the door of the hearts of men. *Inside Out* is all about an inward strength that manifests victorious living in our lives that others will see and want.

When the Holy Spirit gets on the inside of us, His glory shines on the outside. Not only will others be affected, but also we will experience change in our own lives. Too often today we find legalism working on the outside, killing what is on the inside, and leaving people stuck in predicaments that bind them in their souls. When Jacob asked Isaac to bless him, he did not request an outward blessing. He did not ask Isaac for his livestock or gold. He asked him for a blessing that was not on the surface. In Genesis 27:19 Jacob said to Isaac: "Please arise, sit and eat of my game [venison], that your soul may bless me."

Jacob wanted more than what his father possessed materially. He wanted what was inside Isaac. He knew that if he could have what his father had on the inside, then he could also have everything else. When we seek the heart of the Father and want what is *in God*, we can have all that is His. On the other hand, when we allow God access to all that is *in us*, then He has all of us!

> ## RENEWAL OF THE MIND IS RECONSTRUCTION OF THE SOUL.

In the process of obtaining a bachelor's degree in criminology from Florida State University, I studied about the power of an inside job. When crimes are committed with unquestionable perfection, detectives conclude, "This had to be an inside job!" Whether it is due to a positive or negative tip, an inside job gets the work done. Jesus would have never made it to the cross if it had not been for Judas's inside job. The spies would have never completed their Jericho mission if it were not for Rahab's inside job.

God wants to do an inside job on the inner man! Renewal of the mind is reconstruction of the soul. If all of us would humble ourselves and be honest, we would all admit that we could use a little remodeling of the soul.

I have been doing Greek and Hebrew word studies for more than twenty years. It has been very beneficial to my warfare and deliverance ministry. The more that I dig into the root meanings of words and focus on paying attention to detail, the greater the results that I receive. I have created a list that provides Greek words for the states of the soul, which I believe you will find is a useful reference for you as you read this book. Take a few minutes to review this list now before you continue reading.[2]

STATES OF THE SOUL

GREEK TERM	STRONG'S NUMBER	DEFINITION
Psuche	5590	The part of man held in common with animals; the part of man that is conscious of the environment
Psuchos	5592	The act of breathing or to blow cold air
Psucho	5594	To breathe cool air
Psuchomai		To grow spiritually cold
Kauson	2742	Burning heat
Psuchros	5593	Neither hot or cold; of no good quality
Zestos	2200	To be on fire for God
Anapsucho	404	To make cool and refresh
Apopsucho	674	To be faint in heart
Ekpsucho	1634	To die
Katapsucho	2596 + 5594	To cool off
Pneuma	4151	The spirit (breath), which is the part of man that animals do not have in common. They do not possess a spirit (*pneuma*), which is the avenue by which man communicates with God.
Pneumatikos	4153	When the spirit of man is governed under the divine order of God

STATES OF THE SOUL

GREEK TERM	STRONG'S NUMBER	DEFINITION
Soma	4983	The actual body of man
Sarx	4561	Flesh
Sunesis	4907	That which gives man the ability to put facts together and have knowledge and understanding (intellect)
Anthropos	444	Man
Apsuchos	895	Lifeless
Dipsuchos	1374	Double minded (two-souled)
Isopsuchos	2473	Like-minded
Oligopsuchos	3642	To have a little soul or be of a little spirit; fainthearted; fearful
Sumpsuchos	4861	To be joined at the soul (soul tie)
Psuchikos	5591	The carnality of man in relations with the fallen state of man
Sarkikos	4559	The carnality of the flesh
Psuchikon		The body governed by a soul under the power of a fallen instinct
Kardia	2588	The heart as the seat of life
Dianoia	1271	Understanding
Zoe	2222	Life in God as a principle

STATES OF THE SOUL

GREEK TERM	STRONG'S NUMBER	DEFINITION
Bios	979	Possessions in life, or life as it relates to scientific study
Biosis	981	How a person spends his or her life
Agoge	72	How a person conducts him or herself in life
Nous	3563	The mind as the seat of reflective consciousness
Hule	5208	Matter

Before reading the following chapters, let's pray this prayer together:

Father God, I thank You for Your engrafted Word. Lord, I give You permission to renovate any room in my life that needs to be made new. Breathe Your *pneuma* into my being. I receive *zoe life* and confess that *bios life* will never rule over it. As I read the pages of this book, I thank You for a spiritual encounter that will bring *dianoia* (understanding). As a result of this, the *biosis* (timing) and the *agoge* (right conduct) of my life will be well pleasing in Your sight. I declare that my life is not governed by *psuchikon* (carnality). Instead I get under the order of *pneumatikon* (God's spiritual order) so that Your kingdom may manifest Your will in my life. I renounce *oligopsuchos*; I am not small-minded, and I do not have a little spirit. I am not fainthearted or fearful. I am *isopsuchos* (one with God), and I agree with Your plan for my destiny. Also, I renounce the spirit of *ekpsuchos* (death), dipsuchos (double-mindedness), psuchros (lukewarmness), and all sumpsuchos (soul ties). I am zestos (on fire) for You, Lord, and I will never open the doors to psuchomai (to grow cold). In Jesus's name I pray, amen!

I pray that through the contents of this book you will allow God to do an *inside job* on you. I also pray that it will cause a domino effect in the lives of many others. If there is anything manifesting in your consciousness or hiding behind your subconsciousness, allow the words of this book to deal with it from the inside out. Enjoy!

chapter 1

INNER HEALING—MINISTRY
TO THE WHOLE MAN

ECENTLY THE LORD has caused the subject of inner healing to weigh heavily upon my heart. There is a desperate need for it in the body of Christ. Inner healing gives us the ability to draw closer to God. Because we are living in days of apostasy, many will become offended and fall away. They will consider themselves to have fallen away *only* from the church, but they have deceptively fallen away from God! I believe key reasons for this are their wounded spirits and their need for inner healing.

It is important for me to release what God wants me to release in the atmosphere concerning ministry to the whole man. People need ministry to the whole man! There has been a great divide between deliverance and inner healing ministries. It is my prayer that this book will bridge that gap. Some deliverance ministers believe people need only to have demons cast out of them. On the other side, some inner healing ministers believe that only inner healing is needed. The answer to this problem of division is *balance*. Neither side is right or wrong concerning this issue. No special interest group in ministry can corner the market on salvation and deliverance by limiting it just to what they do. People who have been traumatically oppressed by demons need inner healing. Many leaders are burned out from counseling people who continually have the same issues, never finding victory. People need the full gospel to receive ministry to the whole man.

When the full gospel is released, fitly joined together, the ministry gifts of God can get on the front lines and destroy the powers of the enemy. Salvation will be inevitable! (Please note that in systematic theology, "salvation" denotes the whole process by which man is delivered from all that would prevent his attaining to the highest good that God has prepared for him.[1])

Salvation includes:

+ Deliverance
+ The infilling of the Holy Ghost
+ The ministry of casting out devils
+ Inner healing ministry
+ Spiritual discipline and maintenance
+ Discipleship

The six ingredients of salvation listed above help believers get in place to experience all that God has for them. We will take a look at each of these components in this chapter. All of these ingredients are needed for salvation, but I would like to highlight the need for inner healing ministry. I believe that inner healing seals the deal in the deliverance process. Deliverance has leaked out of the lives of many because inner healing was not combined with deliverance. Understanding the important role of inner healing will combat backsliding. Backsliding is not an option to a man or woman who is whole.

WHAT IS INNER HEALING?

What is inner healing ministry? It is important to first know why we need inner healing. Man was created as a spirit. He lives in a body, and he possesses a soul. The war in the spirit realm takes place to gain control of the body, which is God's creation.

The spirit of man makes contact with the world through the body. Without a body we would float around in eternity. Our flesh suit is the only thing that holds us down in the world. The flesh is also what keeps us from being able to see into the spirit realm. Humanity is constantly in a struggle between the soul and the spirit for control of the body. Romans 6:16 warns us that whatever we yield our members to—sin or obedience—is what we will serve. The soul wants to control our bodies with its carnal desires. On the other hand, the Holy Spirit, in our spirit, wants to control our bodies to glorify God in the earth realm.

The truth is that our flesh can never be saved, and the only way we can deal with it is to kill it. We must die to the flesh and *make it* submit to the will of God! The Book of James counsels us to submit to the will of God by resisting the devil. This literally means to come up against him. We cannot work *with* the devil! We must flow in the opposite direction of his bidding. The Bible teaches that witchcraft is a work of the flesh (Gal. 5:19–20). Demons operate in the lives of believers through the flesh realm. (See chapter 2 regarding the five realms related to this book.)

The Word of the Lord tells us that believers are seated in heavenly places with Jesus (Eph. 2:6). Just like anything else in faith, this position is not given to us automatically just because we repeat the sinner's prayer. A believer's faith must be activated in the truth to stand against the lies of the dark realms. Every realm outside of the realm of the Holy Spirit is a dark realm. Dark realms work against believers to make sure they do not tap into the realm of light where Jesus is Lord!

> **WE CANNOT WORK *WITH* THE DEVIL! WE MUST FLOW IN THE OPPOSITE DIRECTION OF HIS BIDDING.**

Where is the believer in the midst of all this? Remember, we are spirits created in the image of God, and we possess souls. The soul is the part of us that is eternal and will go to heaven or hell. The body, which is only a temporary earth suit, will go back to the dust from which it came. Both sides of the soul (good and evil) want to use the body to serve its purpose in the earth. The only way this can happen is to control the mind or the soul of a man. This is why we hear about people selling their souls to the devil. Wherever the soul goes, the body will follow! If the mind of a man can be controlled, his steps can be led.

This is why God wants our minds renewed. If our minds are renewed, the body will follow. The Lord orders the steps of a "good" man (Ps. 37:23). The devil understands this, and he will use the natural soul or demonic realm to distract a man from his destiny. These life distractions that get into the soul of a man can affect his spirit.

People often ask, "How can a demon reside in a place where the Holy Spirit abides?" The answer is simple. Demons do not abide in the spirit of anyone—heathens or believers. The spirit of a man is a place reserved for the Holy Spirit alone. However, demons infiltrate the lives of people through the flesh realm. They go through the realm of the flesh to control the soul realm. This is how believers who are filled with the Holy Spirit can find themselves strongly influenced by devils. A devil cannot enter the spirit of a man, but it can control a man to the point where it affects his spirit.

A perfect example is driving a car. It does not matter if I am not in the front seat steering the car as long as I can sit in the backseat and tell the driver where to go. Whether the car is being driven from the wheel or controlled from the backseat, the key word is *influence*. This means that a demon does not have to be in the spirit of a man as long as he has influence over him. The devil is a *backseat driver* in the lives of believers! All he needs is access. This is why God warns us that we cannot give place (access or opportunity) to the enemy (Eph. 4:27). As long as he can control the body (or vehicle) of a believer to do his dirty work in the earth realm, he is satisfied. Proverbs 6:30 tells us that a thief who comes to satisfy his own lust is not despised by others. It is what he exists to do.

The devil hates humanity because it has been made "in the image of God"! Every life that Satan destroys fulfills his greatest desire. Every time the devil sees us, we remind him of God and the place he used to have with God. He is a tormented being with a vengeance directed against the elect of God that can never be fulfilled. It frustrates him when truth gets implanted in the inward part of a man. He knows for a fact that he will not be able to have a part of that life.

Believers must be able to stand before the devil and say, "Satan, you have no part in me!" Inner healing is needed so that believers can be delivered from the residue of their past bondages. Just because a sinful act has ceased does not mean the source of what made that sinful act happen is gone. For this reason many backslide or struggle with subliminal feelings that they dare not discuss. Let's talk about it!

DEALING WITH THE RESIDUE

A very important thing to remember about inner healing is that our bodies were not created to operate in the demonic realm. We were not made to carry devils. Things that people experience through associations and generations leave imprints on their souls and affect their spirits to the point that they need repair. The Bible refers to broken hearts and wounded spirits. Traumatic experiences such as a failed relationship, loss of a loved one, molestation, rejection, ungodly soul ties, witchcraft, abuse, and many more do not go away simply because the person comes out of the situation. That person often is left with subliminal baggage, which grows and moves through life with that person unnoticed.

> INNER HEALING IS NEEDED SO THAT BELIEVERS CAN BE DELIVERED
> FROM THE RESIDUE OF THEIR PAST BONDAGES.

The residual effect of experiences like the ones I mentioned above leaves marks on the lives of many. These marks need special attention, and we call this attention *inner healing*. Many people do not have victory in their lives because they have deep-rooted issues from the past that haunt them. The problem is that most people cannot put their finger on what is wrong. Effective inner healing ministry identifies deep-rooted issues in the lives of people and deals with these issues.

David acknowledged his need for inner healing by saying:

> Behold, I was brought forth in [a state of] iniquity; my mother was sinful who conceived me [and I too am sinful]. Behold, You desire truth in the inner being; make me therefore to know wisdom in my inmost heart.
>
> —Psalm 51:5–6, AMP

He went on to say:

> Create in me a clean heart, O God, and renew a right, persevering, and steadfast spirit within me.
>
> —Psalm 51:10, AMP

In these passages David admitted the generational bondage of his past. He did not operate in a familiar spirit to make his mother out to be what she was not. This is the first step of inner healing—getting real with God! David understood that God dealt with the heart of a man. If your heart is not right with God, your life is not right with Him. David made a powerful statement: "God desires truth in the inner being!" This is so important because lies lock us into spiritual limbo, and we can never move forward in God. It is in Him that we live and move and have our very own being (Acts 17:28).

Without truth in our innermost being, we are not positioned in God correctly. We are nothing if we do not have the truth in our essence. The truth must get down inside of who we really are! Anything else is a work of the flesh, and true healing will not take place. Inner healing ministry helps us to receive inward truth and to know wisdom in our inmost heart. This keeps us close to God.

I plead the blood of Jesus over your mind and pray that you will receive what God has for you and those to whom you are called to minister. I pray that you will receive increase as you read this book and that the spirit of multiplication will come upon you to receive and release the manifold revelation of inner healing. Selah.

chapter 2

THE ESSENCE OF MAN
(PART I)

I BELIEVE THAT UNDERSTANDING better the essence of man will help you have a better understanding of inner healing. We need to know man's true origin and the essence of human nature. To do this, we must study every element of man's existence in relation to the spirit realm, the flesh realm, and the world.

Too often life has been studied and understood from a biological standpoint only. It is urgent that we understand the essence of life the way God created it—by His Spirit! Adam was formed from the earth. Before God blew into his nostrils, he was just a lump of clay. True life came after the *ruwach*, or breath of God, made man a living soul. Life does not exist outside of God. Many are walking around in the world today without Christ. Real life starts after Christ. "Life after Christ" is the definition of the biblical term for *zoe* life. It literally means: "New birth that ignites 'real life' after Jesus comes into the heart of a human being."

Based on this, people who do not have Christ in their life are literally dead men walking in the earth. This is why we must be born again. The opposite of *zoe* life is *bios* life. *Bios* life is life without *zoe*, or life without God. *Zoe* is the God kind of life. Jesus came that we might have life abundantly (John 10:10). The word *might* is *dunamai*, and it means "potential or possible life." This potential life is assured when we allow *zoe* life to rule over *bios* life. Man is flesh, and he must have contact with the world to exist in the natural realm. We must have bios life. The problem sets in when *bios* life rules over *zoe* life. The life of the spirit in God must take priority if we are to experience abundant life. The spirit must come first. The natural must be second class in the life of the born-again believer. We are spirit beings first, and we cannot be bound by the curse of the natural man. The natural man cannot and will not discern the things of the spirit. Where there is no discernment of the things of the spirit, there will be no *zoe* life.

> **WHEN PEOPLE MAKE THEIR OWN GUIDELINES IN LIFE, THEY ARE BOUND TO GET OFF TRACK.**

Bios life relates to biological life or life as it has been scientifically studied. Many understand life only as explained by history or science books. There is only one book that really counts when it comes to the explanation of life—the Bible! The unadulterated Word of God cannot be tampered with. It is the schematic of life, breathed from the lungs of God through submitted vessels into the earth realm. The Masons, Jehovah's Witnesses, and many other groups have fabricated their own books and called them *Bibles*, but the true Word of God cannot be added to or taken away from. It is Spirit!

It amazes me that people who are supposed to be smart have foolish revelations that teach mankind evolved from apes. If you believe in evolution, it is my prayer that this chapter will deliver you from this demonic doctrine of devils. When people make their own guidelines in life, they are bound to get off track.

ZOE LIFE

Let's plunge into the truth about life as God created it—*zoe* life.

The Complete Word Study Dictionary: New Testament refers to a Greek phrase, *psuche zosa.* When this phrase is broken down into two parts, it brings great revelation:[1]

- *Psuche* means "soul life."
- *Zosa* means "living soul."

After the fall of Adam, men had only *soul life.* This is the fallen state of man, existing without God. This is why Jesus is called the *second Adam* (1 Cor. 15:45). He came to restore or get back what the first Adam lost. Jesus came so that we could become living souls. Living souls live, move, and have their being in Christ.

Since the beginning of time the devil has been jealous of man. Satan was cast out of heaven and cursed as a fallen angel. His destiny is inevitable, and one day he will be on eternal lockdown in the bottomless pit. God did not give him another chance. Yet today some preachers, even some Pentecostal preachers, support ministries of inclusion that even teach that the devil will be forgiven. The Bible says that in the last days even the elect will be deceived (Matt. 24:24). This is the greatest deception I have ever heard of. If the devil will be saved, why is there a need for a plan for salvation? Not only is this teaching a deception, but it is also a joke. God is laughing at these teachers of falsehood! When men attempt to proclaim that they know more than God, God will turn them over to foolishness.

The objective of Satan's existence is to make man fall (with him). He is deceived to think that he can get back at God by destroying what is closest to God's heart—humanity.

The Fall

The Bible teaches that the devil was cast out of heaven for merchandising (Ezek. 28:16). Have you ever wondered whom the devil was merchandizing with? It takes a *seller* and a *buyer* to merchandise. If the devil was selling, who was doing the buying? Surely the angels did not need to buy anything. There could be no merchandising in heaven! When I studied the word *merchandising*, I discovered that the literal meaning is "to traffic." As an ex–drug dealer, it is easy for me to understand that term. To *traffic* is to travel from one place to another to provide something that is illegal to a customer. Who were Lucifer's customers?

If we are to understand man's true essence, we must start by knowing that Adam and Eve were not the first beings to walk the earth. I believe that there was a pre-Adamic race. Please do not panic. Give me a chance to break it down. My explanation is surely better than the *bios* theory…coming from apes!

Breaking It Down

First, we must understand that there is a battle going on in the spirit. The war that broke out in heaven is not over. The battle is over who will control or possess the souls of men. While in the earth realm, wherever the soul or the spirit leads, the body will follow. Whoever controls the body on the earth can have the soul of a spirit in eternity. I cannot say it enough—each of us is a spirit, possesses a soul, and lives in a body.

When all is said and done, the body will return to the dust of the earth from which it came. Then the spirit (the real man) will go into the realm of eternity (heaven or hell) based on the life lived on the earth. The spirit of a man possesses a soul (mind, will, intellect, and emotions). Whether we go to heaven or hell, we will take all of these qualities with us.

HELL IS REAL

We will never mentally or emotionally die.

Some people report that in the early seventies, a group of scientists were studying activity in the earth's core. They drilled thousands of miles into the center of the earth and began to pick up strange noises on their microphones. As they listened closer they realized it was the sound of tormented souls![2] I believe that this account could be accurate.

We will never mentally or emotionally die. And the Bible clearly tells us that if we do not choose eternity in heaven by accepting the salvation God offers through Jesus Christ, the only other option is eternity in hell. (See 1 John 5:13; Matthew 5:22, 29–30.) Although there are many people who do not believe in the existence of hell— including some who teach from the pulpit that hell does not exist—the Bible is very explicit in its teaching about the reality of hell. (See Luke 16:23–28.) Jesus describes the horrors of hell as "everlasting fire" (Matt. 25:41). We learn from the Book of Revelation that for those condemned to hell, "the smoke of their torment ascends forever and ever; and they have no rest day or night" (Rev. 14:11).

The Bible tells us that hell is in the center of the earth. (See Matthew 12:40; Ephesians 4:9.) Scientists have confirmed that the center core of the earth is hot—at least 12,000 degrees Fahrenheit hot![3] *Whew!*

Some say that God loves us too much to send us to hell. I say that God loves us so much, rather than allowing the devil to have us, He created hell. He is a jealous God! And He allowed His own Son to be put to death for our sins so that a plan of salvation would be available to every person. If we accept His salvation, we will never be condemned to an eternity in hell. But if we do not accept Him, we will be "cast into the lake of fire" which is hell (Rev. 20:15).

I love the Lord! I pray that you love Him too as you are reading this book. Do you believe in heaven, hell, and the judgment of God? If you do not, pay close attention to what I am about to say. The torments of hell are so bad that not even Hitler would want a Jew to go there. It is the place where the worm does not die. For those who transition to the other side of life without a revelation of *zoe* life...it is a terrible thing. A cliché says that a mind is a terrible thing to waste. Let me edit that saying this way: "A soul (mind) is a terrible thing to lose." The most terrible thing about hell is the realization that a person has been deceived. In hell it is too late to receive *zoe*! In hell, there is no second chance from the caverns of the pit.

Let me take a moment to reach out to the backslidden preacher in the pulpit, the lukewarm mother on the front row, and the teenagers who are playing church to appease their parents. Hell is real! I would like to also reach out to the atheist, agnostic, unsaved scientists, and any others who are bound by *bios* life and feel that they do not need God. Jesus loves you; do not be deceived.

I would also like to reach out to Muslims, Jehovah's Witnesses, Masons, Shriners, Alphas, Kappas, Eastern Stars, and any other groups that abide under a closed heaven. I bind the spirits that would close heaven to you and give you a one-way ticket to hell. Be judged now, or the judgment at the end will be too hard to bear. If you want to make heaven and miss hell, pray this prayer with me:

> *Father God, in the name of Jesus, I believe in the Holy Trinity. I believe that the Father sent the Son so that the Holy Spirit could live on the inside of me. I believe in heaven and hell. I choose heaven! I renounce every religion, group, doctrine, or*

belief system that would hinder my faith in Jesus. Jesus, I receive You as Savior of my life. I give you permission to be Lord. Lord, You came that I may have abundant (zoe) life, and I receive it. Satan, I renounce your deception, and I cast down your lies. You are a defeated foe in my life. I choose Jesus over you. Jesus, lead me to a place of fellowship where I can learn to serve and grow in You. I thank You for delivering me from demonic association and infiltration. I praise You for filling me with Your Holy Spirit so that I can experience victorious living in You. In Jesus's name, amen.

Satan and His Demonic Realm of Influence

When our bodies die, we will become acutely aware of what true life is all about. Depending on the lives we lived in the flesh, we will consciously experience one of two eternities—eternal bliss in heaven or eternal torment in the pit. To get a revelation of these realities, we must discuss realms.

There are five realms I would like to identify for the purposes of this book:

1. Flesh realm
2. Demonic spirit realm
3. Soul realm
4. Natural realm
5. Holy Spirit realm

A *realm* is actually a sphere, kingdom, or domain of authority. Every realm listed above has its own kingdom, and every kingdom has a king. Every king rules in his realm, and the dominion of that king is limited to that realm only—with only one exception! Jesus is the Lord of lords and the King of kings over all these realms! He holds dominion in every realm. Despite this, there are strongmen that rule in every realm. They are counterfeit lords. The strongman that rules in each of these realms is listed below:

+ Flesh realm—the flesh is lord.
+ Demonic realm—Satan is lord.
+ Soul realm—the mind is lord.
+ Natural realm—the world is lord.
+ Holy Spirit realm—*Jesus is Lord.*

The realm to which we submit our lives is the realm to which we are bound for service. We actually become prisoners of that realm. For the born-again believer who has submitted to the lordship of Christ, the Holy Spirit lives within that person's spirit. That person is, as Paul asserts in Acts 20:22, "bound" by the Spirit of the Lord. This is a godly bondage whereby we submit our members to do the will of the Lord in the earth realm. This is how we can be in the world but not of the world.

> **DEPENDING ON THE LIVES WE LIVED IN THE FLESH, WE WILL CONSCIOUSLY EXPERIENCE ONE OF TWO ETERNITIES—ETERNAL BLISS IN HEAVEN OR ETERNAL TORMENT IN THE PIT.**

On the other hand, when we submit ourselves to the earth realm, we are bound by all the things of the world, which are:

+ "The lust of the flesh"
+ "The lust of the eyes"
+ "The pride of life" (1 John 2:16)

Satan lords over the dark realm of the demonic. Darkness reigns in realms where there is no light and no truth. In the Bible, Satan is identified as the god of this world and the lord of the earth realm (2 Cor. 4:4). It is important to know that the worldly realm and the flesh realm work hand in hand. Though there is a "spirit of the world," Satan lords over it through the demonic realm. The world, the flesh, and the satanic are always in agreement.

Let me make a serious statement—the flesh cannot be saved. It must die! When the things of the world and the things of the flesh collide, carnality is born. Carnality is the life of the flesh that gets its pleasures from the things of this world. It is devilish! Since the fall of man, Satan has been given the legal right and authority to be lord of the world. The only way he can enforce his lordship in the life of a human being is through the flesh realm.

God gave mankind a precious gift—a will. Man has a choice as to what he does with his flesh, and thus is lord over his flesh. But when man chooses unwisely and fails to allow the lordship of Christ to reign in his life, the devil will automatically usurp authority. I feel safe in saying that even though man was given dominion and has a will, how he uses that will gives either God or the devil rulership over him. We can see how this works by taking a close look at the example of Adam and Eve.

NAKED AND ASHAMED

Before Adam and Eve ate the forbidden fruit, they were submissive to God. The Bible says that they were naked even before they fell. But after they fell, they suddenly had an awareness of their nakedness that was not originally there. The *bios* that I spoke of earlier came into existence, which is an awareness of the physical life, of life apart from God. It denotes man's ability to relate to and know things outside of God. It was rooted in the demonic. The devil told Eve, "You can be like God." In other words, he told Eve, "You can know what God knows." This caused Adam and Eve to take on a new kind of nakedness. Since that time, the scientific genius of men has attempted to know more than God.

Let us take a look at the two kinds of nakedness discussed in Genesis 3. The nakedness before sin and the nakedness after sin differ, and each must be addressed.

> Then the eyes of both of them were opened, and they knew that they were naked; and they sewed fig leaves together and made themselves coverings. And they heard the sound of the Lord God walking in the garden in the cool of the day, and Adam and his wife hid themselves from the presence of the Lord God among the trees of the garden.
>
> —Genesis 3:7–8

Before they fell, Adam and Eve had walked before God naked. This kind of nakedness means to be open before God. They had nothing to hide and walked in the peace of His presence. This peace was interrupted by disobedience. The nakedness (after sin) caused Adam and Eve to try to hide from God. The Bible teaches that rebellion is like witchcraft (1 Sam. 15:23). Witchcraft displaced their peace!

The nakedness (after sin) is defined as "ashamed before God." When we sin, our flesh hides from the presence of God in shame. Let's define the two words for "naked" in the Hebrew:

1. The naked before sin is `arowm; it means "nude or naked, not clothed, or uncovered."

2. The naked after sin is `eyrom, and it comes from the root word `aram, which means "subtle and crafty. This

means to be stripped before God to put on the nature of the devil.

After Adam and Eve fell, they took on the spirit of the one to whom they yielded their flesh. Whomever we yield our flesh to is the one we will serve. Adam and Eve took on the Luciferian spirit, or the spirit that causes one to fall from God. The Luciferian spirit started in Lucifer's revolt in heaven, then it moved through the Garden of Eden, and it rules over regions in the world today. The only motive of the Luciferian spirit is to draw men away from God and to cause them to fall. Men must be first drawn away from God to ultimately fall.

The Bible says there will be a great falling away (2 Thess. 2:3). This is called the *apostasy*. The apostasy occurs when men who have a relationship with God fall away from the faith.

Adam and Eve took on a flesh covering, a new order, and became subject to God. Through their rebellion, they gave room to Satan to have dominion in the earth realm. This new flesh that they took on is defined as the *pudendum* of a man. The word *pudendum* means "to expose the private parts." Adam and Eve were exposed to private parts or secrets. The word *occult* means "secret." Through sin, the occult entered the earth realm.

Wearing chains around the neck with an upside-down demonic cross on it, wearing black, or having tattoos is not what make people subject to the occult. It is man's shame and secrets they hide behind the *fig leaves* of life, causing men to run from God, that promote the occult. The occult causes men to have breaches in their spirits. These people live their lives wondering why something is always missing in their lives.

The Bible declares that everything hidden will be brought to the light (Mark 4:22). Secrets are kept in places of darkness. This is why organizations like the Masons, Shriners, Eastern Star, and other fraternities and sororities are illegal in the eyes of God. It is impossible to live victoriously in Jesus while making dark vows to people, places, and things. It is idolatry! I could explain the spiritual violations of being involved in organizations like this, but it is not the vision of this chapter. Instead I challenge you to always judge the fruit that these groups bear, and it will be easy to identify those groups that are not of God.

We cannot be delivered from things that we will not allow the light to shine on. Problems set in when dark secrets are covered up too long. Many people live their lives in an emotional mess because they have kept secrets too long. The darkness of the secret rules over their heads, and they have no relief.

It is vital to your faith to find someone with whom you can trust the darkest secrets of your life. Accept godly counsel from someone who can give you an ear to hear and a shoulder to lean on. There is safety in counsel because it soothes the mind and deals with the darkness that lurks behind *the spirit of the secret*. There are many who attempt to hide from God even from the pews of a church or the position or title they hold in the church or world.

> **WE CANNOT BE DELIVERED FROM THINGS THAT WE WILL NOT ALLOW THE LIGHT TO SHINE ON.**

But just as Adam and Eve could not hide from God behind the aprons of leaves they made in the Garden of Eden, you will not be able to hide from God behind your family leaves. Have you heard God asking, "Where are you?" Don't you know that God sees everything?

He is really asking: "Where are you in the spirit? I can't find you in your secret."

INHABITANTS OF THE LAND (THE PRE-ADAMIC RACE)

I have personally heard many great leaders teach on the gap theory. It is just that…a theory, but I believe it. Understanding the possibility of what happened between Genesis 1:1 and Genesis 1:2 has helped me to have a better understanding of demonic realms.

In the Book of Genesis, God told Adam to replenish the earth. To replenish means to make complete again or to restock or restore. It means to refill to previous state. Based on this, I believe that God was telling Adam to get the earth back to a state that it was in before. I believe that something cataclysmic happened between Genesis 1:1 and Genesis 1:2. In Genesis 1:1 God created the heavens and the earth. The Amplified Version says that He "prepared, formed," and "fashioned" the earth. In Genesis 1:2 the Bible teaches that the earth was a waste. It was void and without form. How could God form the earth and all of a sudden it become a waste and without form? Something happened! I believe that this was when the earth was frozen in the ice age. This is the age that the dinosaurs walked on Earth. Museums prove that they existed because of the fossil images that are on display. Many theologians have addressed this gap theory (between Genesis 1:1 and Genesis 1:2). Science does not have the answer to this mystery because it cannot be discerned with a natural eye. To understand the essence of man, we must have an eye in the spirit. Inner healing goes to the root of man's essence, but even that comes from the roots of his existence.

I mentioned earlier in this chapter that Lucifer was cast out of heaven because of his merchandising. What kind of merchandising is going on in heaven? There was none and never will be any. There was, however, a connection between Lucifer and the inhabitants of the land, or the pre-Adamic race. This is the race that caused Lucifer to fall and become the prince of darkness, the devil himself. Lucifer fell because of his merchandising with the beings before Adam and Eve. The word *merchandising* means to traffic or make trade. Iniquity was found in Lucifer's heart as he wanted not just to be "like God," but to be God! He wanted to be worshiped by the inhabitants of the earth. As a result of his rebellion, a war broke out in heaven. A third of the angels in heaven rebelled and were booted out with Lucifer. God didn't give them a second chance as He did with mankind. When Lucifer was cast out of heaven, I believe that this is when all of the earth was frozen. What a fall to cause all of creation to freeze up! It is called the ice age. There is not a generation that can be traced back to this time, but even science confirms it. Dinosaur fossils prove that the earth froze so quickly that animals died with food in their mouths. I believe that the flood during Noah's time was not the first time God had dealt with the earth in massive judgment. This answers so many questions. The entire earth was annihilated, and it became without form. The inhabitants of the earth (at that time) were destroyed. They were not human beings created in the image of God. There was no heaven and hell destination for them. They were banished to roam the earth without bodies forever. These are the demons that possess the bodies of men today. They need a body to live in! They are demon spirits that seek dry places. In the demonic realm demons spirits fall under two categories:

1. Demons—inhabitants of the land (pre-Adamic race). These spirits need a body to live in. These are the demons that we cast out of people, and they are tormented without a host.

2. Fallen angels—angels that rebelled with Lucifer.
   Example: A principality does not need a body. They rule over cities and regions.

I know that this teaching takes soaking in the spirit to conceive. Your mind has to be renewed because this message is not popular. In the dealing with the issue of the inhabitants of the land, degeneration must be understood.

SPIRITUAL DEGENERATION

> But when the unclean spirit has gone out of a man, it roams through dry [arid] places in search of rest, but it does not find any. Then it says, I will go back to my house from which I came out. And when it arrives, it finds the place unoccupied, swept, put in order, and decorated. Then it goes and brings with it seven other spirits more wicked than itself, and they go in and make their home there. And the last condition of that man becomes worse than the first. So also shall it be with this wicked generation.
> —Matthew 12:43–45, AMP

This passage teaches on the degeneration of man. The word for wicked is *poneria*, and it means to worsen in state. Though things in life occur that affect people in a negative way, it is the continual cycle of the exiting and entering of demons in a person's body that causes degeneration. James made a reference to people who had confusion operating in their lives: "The reason there is so much confusion around you is because there is so much confusion in you." (See James 3:13–14.) Confusion roots itself in the life of a person through demonic presence. It deteriorates the state of a man, and that person gets progressively more degenerate—spiritually, mentally, emotionally, and even physically.

Darkness is the main ingredient of spiritual deterioration. The root word for confusion is *confuse*, which means to be unclear, indistinct, and to have no clarity. Other words given in relation to being confused are *opaque* and *obscure*. These are key words to make my point about degeneration.

The Bible speaks of the eyes of some men being full of darkness (Luke 11:34). This word *darkness* is *skoteinos* in the Greek, and it means to be so full of darkness that vision becomes opaque and obscure. It goes on further in meaning to become a "blockhead" due to the spiritual blindness caused by the effects of darkness. Degeneration causes the state of a man to continually grow worse.

God made man in His image. We are the apple of His eye, and He is constantly mindful of us. This is why the devil hates us—we look like God! Without inner healing, our image is distorted, and we start looking like the lies of the enemy.

The Book of Psalms asks, "What is man that You are mindful of him?" (Ps. 8:4). Well, to begin, we are the created beings to whom God gave a second chance. He did not give the devil another chance. He did not give the angels that fell with the devil another chance. I thank the Lord that I know Him as the God who gave me another chance!

He did not give me another chance for me to become depressed and downtrodden. I do not live just in the earth realm—I live in Him! It is a miserable thing to live in this earth outside of God. When we do this, we neglect to take advantage of our second chance.

When Adam and Eve walked with God before the Fall, they were in a place where anxiety and failure could not abide. You and I walk in this place when we are open before God. God created Adam and Eve because He was looking for somebody to fellowship with. But Adam and Eve broke that fellowship, and the fruit of broken fellowship with God is misery.

This is why the spirit of a man must be regenerated. Being born again or regenerated in God restores our fellowship with God and opens the door for the power of the miseries of life to be removed far away from us. I declare that the spirit of the roller coaster is being broken off the lives of those who will get in place to receive it. No more "one minute you are up and the next minute you are down" syndrome! No more yo-yo or seesaw experiences!

In the name of Jesus, I bind the power of being double minded. The Bible says that a double-minded man is unstable in all of his ways. The Amplified Version calls it "of two minds" (James 1:8). I believe that these two spirits of double-mindedness represent the one that wants to do right and the one that wants to do wrong. There is the spirit of light and the spirit of darkness.

> BEING BORN AGAIN OR REGENERATED IN GOD RESTORES OUR FELLOWSHIP WITH GOD AND OPENS THE DOOR FOR THE POWER OF THE MISERIES OF LIFE TO BE REMOVED FAR AWAY FROM US.

The Holy Ghost is in your spirit, but the devil operates in the kingdom of the flesh. The flesh is where we reign as kings in our own lives. As David did, we must repent for taking counsel in our own soul (Ps. 13:2). People who lord over their own lives will definitely suffer affliction of the soul. Emotional bondage stems from wrong choices made in life. Repent if you have been your own lord! Allow Him to be the center of your joy and the Lord of your very essence. In doing this, your existence will be fulfilled.

chapter 3

THE ESSENCE OF MAN
(PART II)

THE FOURTH CHAPTER of Hebrews brings even more clarification about the essence of man. In verses 12–16, we read:

For the word of God is living and powerful, and sharper than any two-edged sword, piercing even to the division of soul and spirit, and of joints and marrow, and is a discerner of the thoughts and intents of the heart. And there is no creature hidden from His sight, but all things are naked and open to the eyes of Him to whom we must give account. Seeing then that we have a great High Priest who has passed through the heavens, Jesus the Son of God, let us hold fast our confession. For we do not have a High Priest who cannot sympathize with our weaknesses, but was in all points tempted as we are, yet without sin. Let us therefore come boldly to the throne of grace, that we may obtain mercy and find grace to help in time of need.

The Amplified Version of Hebrews 4:15 reads, "We do not have a High Priest Who is unable to understand and sympathize and have a shared feeling with our weaknesses and infirmities and liability to the assaults of temptation." Jesus came to the earth so that He could experience every trauma and negative emotion that we could possibly ever experience. He (like man) was a spirit, He lived in a body, and He possessed the soul. In other words, we cannot tell Jesus that He does not understand what we are going through.

Jesus left His throne and walked the earth as a human being. When Jesus was pierced in His side, though He was God, it hurt! He took on our sicknesses and infirmities on the cross. No one in the last stages of AIDS can say that He does not know how they feel. Cancer patients, crack addicts, the brokenhearted, and anyone else going through the worst things that can happen in life can rest assured that Jesus has been there, done that too! He took on all sickness, sin, and every assignment from hell on the cross.

Hebrews 4:13 states that no creature exists that is concealed or hidden from God's sight. They are exposed and defenseless before Him. In the previous chapter we discussed nakedness before God (before and after sin). Hebrews 4:13 takes nakedness before God to another level. It shows us that whether we come clean with God or not, we stand naked before Him. The Greek word for *naked* is *gumnos*, which means to be "without clothing…clad in undergarments only (the outer garments or cloak being laid aside) of the soul [our own mind]…stripped of the body…lay bare."[1]

Standing before God, our flesh looks like dust. He sees the essence of what flesh is made of. Flesh can only deceive man, not God! He discerns all of our thoughts and the intents of our heart. When it is all said and done, we lay bare before the Lord, and He deals with who we really are. The only thing we stand before God with is our soul. We will stand as spirits, possessing a soul that has determined our eternal destiny. We are really not what we have acted out in our flesh suits. When the flesh dies, it goes back to the earth that it came out of. Our only connection with the world is the flesh. It is the avenue that connects the natural to the supernatural, and the barricade that separates man from God. This is why soul and spirit must be severed for man to spend eternity with God.

THE ONLY THING WE STAND BEFORE GOD WITH IS OUR SOUL.

Let's look at Hebrew 4:12 in the Amplified Version:

> For the Word that God speaks is alive and full of power [making it active, operative, energizing, and effective]; it is sharper than any two-edged sword, penetrating to the dividing line of the breath of life (soul) and [the immortal] spirit, and of joints and marrow [of the deepest parts of our nature], exposing and sifting and analyzing and judging the very thoughts and purposes of the heart.

SEPARATION OF SPIRIT AND SOUL

The first thing we need to see is that God wants the spirit and soul separated. *Spirit* is defined as "the immortal man that exists in eternity forever." *Soul* is defined as "the breath of life that God breathed into man to give the dirt that he was made out of the ability to exist."

It is clear that the two are different, and they must be separated. This can only be done by the precision of the Word of God. It is the only tool sharp enough to divide the soul and spirit.

Witchcraft has its roots in the attempts of a person to use his or her mind to control the spirit. There are many who tap into the demonic realm through extensive meditation, which is a way of controlling the spirit with the mind. This is the way of darkness. The way of light is recognizing that God meant for the soul and spirit to be severed. This is the only way the mind can be renewed. As the Word of God enters, it separates that which is of the spirit from that which is of mind, will, intellect, and emotions.

> The spirit of man [that factor in human personality which proceeds immediately from God] is the lamp of the Lord, searching all his innermost parts.
>
> —Proverbs 20:27, AMP

The inner man (the spirit man) is literally the essence of who we really are. We are spiritual beings. When we receive the Holy Spirit, He abides in our spirit. Our spirit must come into agreement with the Holy Spirit. Either we will believe the lies of the devil and be damned, or we will come into agreement with the Holy Spirit and be saved. The battle is over the soul. We do not have a right to think as we please. This is the bottom line of the battle.

Let me paint a picture for you. Chrysler is a manufacturer of cars. This company understands the makeup of its cars because they build them from scratch. Let's pretend that your *mind is the engine* of a vehicle, your *will is the steering wheel*, and your *intellect is the fuel*. Your *emotions are the fuel injection system*.

1. The steering wheel determines where that car goes. Jesus said, "Not My will, but Yours, be done" (Luke 22:42). This is the part of us that makes decisions in life. Godly counsel and direction are precious things. Turning down the wrong road could cause breakdowns or major accidents that are hard to recover from.

2. The intellect is the fuel. Intellect is not bad, but how you use your intellect can be bad. It's the weight that you allow your intellect to carry in your life that counts. It

is a sin to be pridefully smart. The actual word *genius* is related to the word *genie*, and it is demonic. It is great to be bright and witty, but when it exalts itself against the knowledge of God, it becomes dark wisdom.

3. The emotions are the fuel injection system. Let's address the sisters. If you were to check us out, we are more emotional than men in most cases. God made us that way. I believe that the rib that He took out of man had something to do with emotions. That's why you have a woman who will run around church and praise God like she is crazy. It is because we tend to be emotional. The problem sets in when we do not know what to do with all of these emotions. The wires get crossed, and the wrong stuff starts to inject into our minds. The end result is emotional instability or a bumpy ride in life.

4. The mind is the engine. This is the part of the car that makes a car what it is. As a man thinks, so is he (Prov. 23:7). While the steering wheel is leading the way, the emotions are injecting fuel, and the intellect (thoughts) is fueling the engine (mind), the car is either riding smoothly or slowly breaking down. Inner healing causes an overhaul of the engine of man to cause things to run smoother in life.

Whatever is sent to the engine (our minds) determines the quality of life we will live. When the Word of God penetrates the barriers of the carnal mind and allows the truth in, it separates the soul from the spirit. The spirit of a man must be allowed to do what God created it to do. Proverbs 20:27 says that the spirit of a man is the lamp (candle) of the

Lord, and it searches our deepest parts. When the spirit and soul abide together, a shade is placed over the light of God (in us) that allows obscurity to set in. This opens the door to the gray areas in our lives.

Chrysler has a diagnostic system that alerts mechanics to what the actual problem is in a car. The spirit of a man (with the Holy Spirit) can be compared to a diagnostic system that searches the deepest parts of our being to discern problems. Ministers, in this essence, can be related to mechanics; they cannot effectively help hurting people if they are not:

1. Using the right manual—the Word of God
2. Connected to the Manufacturer
3. Able to understand how to minister by the Spirit to the spirit of a man to get to the root of the problem

Deep within the spirit of every man is the answer to problems that make them miserable. When the spirit remains connected with the soul, the searchlight is put out, and men remain in darkness. The Bible warns believers to be careful that the light in them does not become dark (Luke 11:35).

THE HEALING PROCESS BEGINS

When the soul and spirit of a man are separated, the healing process can begin. The searchlight shines bright. Without the separation, the soul will continue to control the spirit in obscurity. The soul is overbearing and usurps authority. The soul (mind) is always at enmity against God. Witches often use their minds to control their spirit or to project their spirit into places that their body does not go. This is called *astral* (spirit) projection. Many people deal with the infiltration of demon spirits and fail to realize that dark attacks also come in the form of a human spirit. The human spirit can travel through spiritual space while connected to the body by what is called the *silver cord*. If this cord is cut, the body will die, and the person will be launched into eternity—on the dark side.

The silver cord is the "cord of life." It attaches the spirit of a man to his natural body. The reason a lot of Christians do not know this is because they are natural men who do not understand the things of the spirit. I know because of experience and because I believe what God says over what man says. I have seen a human spirit (out of a body). Ecclesiastes 12:6 says that we must remember the Creator before the "silver cord" of life is snapped apart.

> **DEEP WITHIN THE SPIRIT OF EVERY MAN IS THE ANSWER TO PROBLEMS THAT MAKE THEM MISERABLE.**

We were created to do supernatural feats for the Lord. The flesh, the devil, and the world form a threefold cord to stop man from doing the greater works that Jesus promised we would be able to do.

I know of people who operate on the dark side to the point that they can climb walls like Spider-Man, walk through walls, and even translate their bodies from one place to the other supernaturally. Dominion was given to mankind, not just Christians. Though it is devilish, many operate in powers outside of God.

On the other hand, when the soul and spirit are divided and a person submits to God, blind eyes will open, the dead will be raised, and lives will be changed.

chapter 4

EXPERIENCING THE FULLNESS
OF SALVATION

I GET VERY EXCITED when I see the Old Testament word for salvation, which is *Yeshuw`ah*. It is another word for Jesus. Glory to God…His name means *salvation*. Everything we need is incorporated in the name of Jesus. This is why we get results when we call on the name of Jesus!

Everything we need is in salvation. In this chapter we are going to take a close look at the ingredients of salvation. It is important to understand the all-encompassing fullness of the salvation offered to us through the sacrifice of Jesus Christ. Leaders with apostolic authority and grace must teach people to get in place to procure it.

Salvation occurs when a person gets in place to experience the *soteria* of God. This is the Greek word for salvation. It includes:

+ Safety
+ Deliverance
+ Health
+ Salvation
+ Aid
+ Prosperity
+ Help
+ Welfare

Another Greek word, *soterion*, describes salvation as our defense. The Greek word *soter* describes the Deliverer Himself, Jesus Christ. He is our *Soter*, our Deliverer!

Deliverance is of a twofold nature. First, it manifests when a person has been brought out of a thing. This is what happened when the children of Israel came out of Egypt. There is what I call "coming out" deliverance! This is when the people of God are released from the powers of a stronghold and removed from under the control of the taskmaster. At this point of salvation, it is a wilderness experience. Though the person is no longer in Egypt, that person has to deal with wilderness spirits that are assigned to keep him or her out of their promised land. Many people do not understand that when they first give their lives to Jesus, they must walk through the wilderness. Things will not be "hunky-dory," and this phase of a new believer's walk with God requires utmost obedience.

The strongman of the wilderness is doubt. Believers must be careful of thoughts that can turn into words that will detour their destinies while they are still in the wilderness. New believers must immediately learn to cast down imaginations and thoughts that will frame their minds with doubt. Doubt leads to murmuring. Murmuring leads to complaining, and complaining leads to bondage. It is important to remember:

1. Thoughts frame minds to control words.
2. Words frame the world to control our destiny.

> **DOUBT LEADS TO MURMURING. MURMURING LEADS TO COMPLAINING, AND COMPLAINING LEADS TO BONDAGE.**

THE PURPOSE OF COMING OUT

There is purpose in coming out of a thing. God does not just bring us out for the sake of doing so! His purpose for bringing us out is so that we can fulfill His will in the earth realm. He has not called us to come out of the bondages of our past to spend the rest of our lives wandering in the wilderness. We are also called to go in! Everyone could not enter into the Promised Land simply because they came out of Egypt. It was reserved for those whose minds had been renewed in the wilderness. Wilderness situations manifest in our lives to renew our minds. When we attempt to *go around* things in life instead of *going through* them, we keep the same mind-sets. The result is that our minds stay unrenewed in the area of life where we are being challenged. The Bible says that Caleb entered into the Promised Land because he had a different spirit. Let us take a look at the scripture:

> Because all those men which have seen my glory, and my miracles, which I did in Egypt and in the wilderness, and have tempted me now these ten times, and have not hearkened to my voice; surely they shall not see the land which I sware unto their fathers, neither shall any of them that provoked me see it: But my servant Caleb, because he had another spirit with him, and hath followed me fully, him will I bring into the land whereinto he went; and his seed shall possess it.
> —Numbers 14:22–24, KJV

This particular word "another" is `acher*, and it means to follow suit with what was next without procrastination or hindrance. The word "spirit" is *ruwach*, which means breath or spirit of God. This is saying that Caleb was not bound by the status quo of the conditions that were coming up against him in the wilderness. He knew how to flow with the spirit of God and move on to what was next! The anointing of *next* is reserved for those who will not be bound in wilderness struggles. There is something great waiting to happen behind every opposition we experience in life. The spirit of God is available for us to ride on the *ruwach* of what God has for us next. This is especially accessible to new believers and those who have just come out. If you are just coming out of something, I encourage you…do not turn back! There is nothing (for you) behind you, and everything God has for you is ahead of you. There may be some tunnels ahead, but there is light on the other side of the tunnel.

Once you have come out of a thing, you are a candidate for anything that has contaminated your life to *come out of you.* This is the second part of the twofold plan of God for deliverance. Many are excited about evangelizing souls and want to become fishers of men. However, they have failed to recognize this one fact—after a fish has been caught, it must be gutted! There is a gutting anointing reserved for those who are not afraid to admit that they have come out of something. Once we have truly come out, including the process of gutting, the devil will be defeated by every word of our testimony. When we tell our testimonies, we open our hearts for new levels of deliverance because there is nothing hidden that the devil can hold over our heads.

I do not understand why the *ministry of purging* has been put on the back burner in the church. It is hard to comprehend that we could actually think that all the messes that we were involved in as unbelievers will simply disappear when we *come out* of the *stuff* of our lives. I am not just talking about occult stuff or stuff from the world. I am also referring to *religious stuff* that has often become a spiritual mess within—and has been there so long that we have become insensitive to the smell. Religious stuff stinks, and it needs to come out!

> **ONCE YOU HAVE COME OUT OF A THING, YOU ARE A CANDIDATE FOR ANYTHING THAT HAS CONTAMINATED YOUR LIFE TO *COME OUT OF YOU*.**

Just because we stop cursing, drinking, or sleeping around does not mean that stuff is not still there. Stuff will lie dormant in our lives when we have a *form of godliness* on the outside but we have denied what is lurking on in the inside. Where the power of God is unable to work—*the devil is getting busy in that wilderness setting.*

When we have taken the first step of deliverance and have come out of sin's bondage into salvation, then we need to continue on to take the second step by cleaning out all of the contamination from that stronghold that existed inside of us. Only then will we experience the supernatural power of God working on the inside of us to give us "exceedingly abundantly above all that we ask or think" (Eph. 3:20).

When this occurs, it helps us to be yielded vessels for the inner healing of God. This inner healing activates the renewal of the mind process. Many believers are stunted in the renewal of the mind process because they have not received inner healing. A renewed mind is what caused Caleb to walk in a different spirit. Because of this he was not denied entrance into the promises of God. Before we receive the promises of God, we must enter into the place that makes it possible. It is impossible to enter into His promises when we are continually stuck in wilderness cycles.

SAFETY

Even when Joshua and Caleb were allowed entrance to the Promised Land, they were made aware that there were giants in the land. Spiritually speaking, giants in the land represent challenges in life. This is what life is all about, challenges! God takes pleasure in sitting on the throne, watching His children face daily challenges and come out of them victoriously.

I believe that God was bored with the way things were when He created man. Based on this, He made things interesting! He gave us promises and allowed enemies to be assigned against every promise. You can rest assured that whenever there is a promise from God, there is a "giant in your land" assigned to hinder it. Rejoice! This is a confirmation that you are on the right track. Stop crying every time a challenge comes your way! How can you be an overcomer if you have nothing to overcome? What conqueror has not conquered? Victory is perfected in the midst of heated battles. The good thing is that when you are on the Lord's side, *you live in the winner's circle!*

King David was promised the throne of Israel, but he had to endure many enemies and much opposition to obtain it. Listed below are twenty-three promises of protection and safety from the Lord. This is included in your salvation and deliverance packet. Confess these scriptures in confidence over you and your loved ones. As you are confessing them, remember that no weapon formed against you will prosper (Isa. 54:17). God created every devil that forms a weapon against you. He is in total control.

Your Deliverance Guarantee Certificate

The angel of the LORD encamps all around those who fear Him, And delivers them.   —Psalm 34:7
A thousand may fall at your side, And ten thousand at your right hand; But it shall not come near you.   —Psalm 91:7

YOUR DELIVERANCE GUARANTEE CERTIFICATE

The name of the LORD is a strong tower;
The righteous run to it and are safe.

—Proverbs 18:10

He shall cover you with His feathers,
And under His wings you shall take refuge.

—Psalm 91:4

You [God] have been my defense
And refuge in the day of my trouble.

—Psalm 59:16

For the LORD God is a sun and shield.

—Psalm 84:11

I will not be afraid of ten thousands of people
Who have set themselves against me all around.

—Psalm 3:6

You are my hiding place and my shield;
I hope in Your word.

—Psalm 119:114

May the LORD answer you in the day of trouble;
May the name of the God of Jacob defend you.

—Psalm 20:1

Call upon Me in the day of trouble;
I will deliver you, and you shall glorify Me.

—Psalm 50:15

YOUR DELIVERANCE GUARANTEE CERTIFICATE

After these things the word of the LORD came to Abram in a vision, saying, "Do not be afraid, Abram. I am your shield, your exceedingly great reward."

—Genesis 15:1

Surely He shall deliver you from the snare of the fowler
And from the perilous pestilence.

—Psalm 91:3

Deliver my soul, O LORD, from lying lips
And from a deceitful tongue.

—Psalm 120:2

In my distress I cried to the LORD,
And He heard me.

—Psalm 120:1

He will not allow your foot to be moved;
He who keeps you will not slumber.

—Psalm 121:3

The LORD is your keeper...
The LORD shall preserve your going out and your coming in
From this time forth, and even forevermore.

—Psalm 121:5, 8

The sun shall not strike you by day,
Nor the moon by night.

—Psalm 121:6

Your Deliverance Guarantee Certificate

If it had not been the LORD who was on our side,
When men rose up against us,
Then they would have swallowed us alive,
When their wrath was kindled against us;
Then the waters would have overwhelmed us.

—Psalm 124:2–4

Our help is in the name of the LORD,
Who made heaven and earth.

—Psalm 124:8

As the mountains surround Jerusalem,
So the LORD surrounds His people
From this time forth and forever.

—Psalm 125:2

Blessed is every one who fears the LORD,
Who walks in His ways.

When you eat the labor of your hands,
You shall be happy, and it shall be well with you.
Your wife shall be like a fruitful vine
In the very heart of your house,
Your children like olive plants
All around your table.
Behold, thus shall the man be blessed
Who fears the LORD.

The LORD bless you out of Zion,
And may you see the good of Jerusalem
All the days of your life.
Yes, may you see your children's children.

Peace be upon Israel!

—Psalm 128:1–6

YOUR DELIVERANCE GUARANTEE CERTIFICATE

Deliver me, O LORD, from evil men; Preserve me from violent men. —Psalm 140:1
As for the head of those who surround me, Let the evil of their lips cover them; Let burning coals fall upon them; Let them be cast into the fire, Into deep pits, that they rise not up again. —Psalm 140:9–10

HEALTH AND LIFE

For months we have been praying health and healing scriptures on our 5:00 a.m. prayer line. We have used the scriptures from Apostle John Eckhardt's Book *Prayers That Rout Demons*.[1] We have literally prayed the scriptures from the Word of God that promise divine health. We have witnessed healings from bone cancer, sugar diabetes, high blood pressure, and many other infirmities.

Many ask if sicknesses and infirmities are demonic. I think that this is the wrong focus. The focus should be on the fact that it is the will of God for us to be healed. The roots of sicknesses and diseases are not always the same, and they must be spiritually discerned. Generally speaking, I guess I could bottom-line sickness by saying that it is not of God, so it must be of the devil. I can testify to the fact that when demons are cast out of people, the individuals receive healing just like in the Bible.

> And when He had called His twelve disciples to Him, He gave them power over unclean spirits, to cast them out, and to heal all kinds of sickness and all kinds of disease.
>
> —Matthew 10:1

It may be hard for you to imagine that a sickness could be rooted in the demonic. If I was sick, I would imagine anything in the Bible that I needed to imagine that would get me healed. I will be honest to say that I cannot answer all the questions concerning early death, sickness, and infirmity among the saints. Only God knows all the mysteries pertaining to life and death. I am not called to figure it out, anyway. I am called to preach healing and deliverance and lay hands on the sick by faith. This is another benefit of salvation (*soteria*), to be healed by every stripe that Jesus bore on His back! We are healed from sickness, disease, and the spirit of death.

I have spent many hours researching things pertaining to the spirit of death and have listed some of the categories included below:

+ Sickness and disease
+ Domestic violence
+ Violent crimes
+ Crib death
+ Suicide
+ Juvenile delinquency
+ Abortion and miscarriage
+ Terrorism
+ Empty shell assaults (this is what has been happening in our schools)
+ Freak accidents
+ Gang violence and initiations
+ Hijackings, robberies, and burglaries
+ Occult sacrifices
+ Organized police and government corruption
+ Drug deals and other organized crimes
+ Generational curses of infirmity and sickness
+ Abuses of the weak and innocent

THE STRONGMEN OF DEATH

- Azrael
- Uriel
- Samael
- Grim Reaper
- Lilith
- Father Time
- Osiris

- Odin
- Hel
- Izanani
- Shemal
- Thanatos
- Kalma
- Hades

SCRIPTURES ON DEATH

- Psalm 68:20
- Psalm 118:18
- Proverbs 5:4–5
- Proverbs 7:27
- Proverbs 8:36
- Proverbs 10:2

- Proverbs 12:28
- Proverbs 13:14
- Proverbs 14:12
- Proverbs 16:25
- Isaiah 28:18
- 1 John 3:14

In your study and prayer time, you should go over these topics on death. Do not be afraid; God has given us the keys to death, hell, and the grave. By having a working knowledge of these spirits, how death manifests itself in our lives, and what the Bible says about death, you will be a stronger intercessor in dealing with warfare against darkness. The key battle in warfare is death against life. We cannot appreciate victory in life until we have a better revelation of what it could have been like. We can understand what life could have been like when we are able to recognize the fruits of death and its manifestations.

PROSPERITY AND WELFARE

I cannot imagine that God would save me and condemn me to walk in poverty and lack. God promises to prosper us and take care of us. This is what welfare is all about—having your needs taken care of. It is not the will of God for the systems of men to be our source. Being a former recipient of food stamps and welfare, I understand the need for assistance, but I believe that the welfare system in America has become a mockery.

The Word of the Lord says that widows and orphans should be taken care of. Our welfare system has created a generation of lazy people who will never fulfill the call of God upon their lives because of a handout. The welfare system works well when people come through it, but there are many who make a career out of it. The welfare system works well for those who need it and have circumstances out of their control. But for those who become bound by slothful spirits, they will lie around and only obtain that which is brought to them. This is what the animal called a *sloth* does. He lies around and only eats what comes within arm's reach of him. If nothing comes within his reach, he will lie there and die. He hangs upside down from trees. So shall it be for those who believe upside-down political doctrines that pretend to give them aid when it actually holds them back. They will die where they lie.

> **IT IS NOT THE WILL OF GOD FOR THE SYSTEMS OF MEN TO BE OUR SOURCE.**

The key to true prosperity is making God our source. The Lord is my Shepherd, *and I shall not be in want.* He promises in 3 John 2: "Beloved, I pray that you may prosper in all things and be in health, just as your soul prospers."

This word *prosper* is *euodoo* in the Greek language. It means to have help on the road to the promise. True prosperity in God is when you can see Him doing it—before it is done! Even though your needs seem greater than your provision, you can see your help on the road to your promise. The old saints used to say, "I can feel my help coming on!" This is what faith is all about—God being your ultimate source in times of great need. With this kind of attitude, you cannot lose! He is your help in times of need.

HELP AND AID

David was a man with many enemies. With the favor of the Lord come many enemies. In Psalm 3:1–2, he spoke of how it seemed as if the numbers of those who troubled him were increased. He recognized that others were saying that there was no help for him in God. This is the taunt of the evil man. He cannot recognize *help in God* because he has none. Everything that he obtains is through trickery, self-gain, competition, and the ways of the world.

Be encouraged; *there is help for you in God.* He is the glory and the lifter of your head. Psalm 10:14 says that even when the wicked condemn God, still He is the helper of the poor and the fatherless. God is the God of our salvation, and He promises to be our help. He hears us and is gracious to us. *He is our helper!* (Ps. 30:10). *HE IS OUR SALVATION!* (Ps. 35:3).

chapter 5

WILL YOU BE MADE WHOLE?

J ESUS ASKED THE lame man at the pool of Bethesda, "Wilt thou be made whole?" (John 5:6, KJV.) It was as if the man had a choice in getting healed. I will be the first to admit that there are many people bound to circumstances that are out of their control. On the other hand, I am convinced that there are others who are bound because of the choices they have or have not made.

The most precious thing God gave man is a will. The definition of the word *will* is "the freedom or power of a person to choose his or her own actions." In the natural and in the spirit there are repercussions when a man is not a good steward of his own volition. When people break natural laws, penalties can range from probation to incarceration and even a death sentence. The Bible states that there is a way that seems right to a man, but the end of it is death. I feel safe in saying that if we do not use our will properly, we will lose it eternally. To use our will outside of the laws of God is sin. Sin always leads to death!

When Jesus addressed the lame man, He was concerned with more than the man's physical condition. Jesus did not offer just healing to his body, but He offered wholeness to every part of his life. The promises of God are manifold. Every promise is funneled from what Christ did on the cross and distributed to every area of need in our lives. Many believers do not understand that it is the Father's delight to see the needs of His children met. And more than that, Ephesians 3:20 teaches that God is able to bless us far above all we can ever ask or think according to the power that works on the inside of us. This word *power* is *dunamis* in the Greek, and it means miracle-working power.

THE POWER OF BELIEVING GOD

There are many powers in the world, but the greatest is the power to *believe God!* Many people run from church service to church service to get a miracle from God. They believe that their healing comes from the gifting of the preacher, but the truth is that their healing resides within their spiritual lives. The potential for everything we need in life has been placed within us through the fullness of salvation from Christ! Jesus said that the enemy comes to steal, kill, and destroy, but He came that we might have abundant life (John 10:10). *Dunamai* is the Greek word for "might," and it means potential or possible power. Ephesians 3:16 tells us that we are "strengthened with might through His Spirit in the inner man." In this verse, the word *might* is *dunamis*, and it means "ability or potential." This is why Ephesians 3:20 refers to "the power working on the inside of us," or the *dunamis*. When we are filled with *dunamis*, the *dunamai* (potential of God's promises) is ignited on the inside of us, and we are in place to receive.

> **EVERY PROMISE IS FUNNELED FROM WHAT CHRIST DID ON THE CROSS AND DISTRIBUTED TO EVERY AREA OF NEED IN OUR LIVES.**

Remember the spies who went in to check out the Promised Land? Only two, Joshua and Caleb, were "well able" (Num. 13:30, KJV). Caleb and Joshua were able not because of some special ability. They were well able because they chose to believe God! When it comes to what God has for us, we cannot go in to receive it with spiritual question marks over our heads. We must know it is ours before we go in, or the doors will be closed to us. We must choose God's best for our lives with a spiritual exclamation mark ruling over our heads. Making the right choices always opens the door to deliverance, healing, prosperity, and the solution for all our needs. For example, the only way a person can be delivered from generational poverty is *by choosing* to walk out of it. Making the right choices in life counts!

The man at the pool of Bethesda had to make a choice, and he made the right one. The words that Jesus spoke ignited the faith in his belly that had not been used for over thirty years. This man had been lying around other folks who had been getting healed, but there was something blocking him from receiving his healing.

RAISE THE WATER LEVELS

Recently God spoke to me about how the water levels of our faith need to be higher so that there will be a proper spiritual flow. This flow will cause a balanced distribution, which will manifest in victorious living in every area of our lives. When these water levels are low, there are areas of our lives in which we suffer lack. For example, I know people who walk in a high level of spiritual authority such as doing warfare and casting out devils. On the other hand, some of them fall short in the area of paying their bills or operating in integrity. Others are able to minister effective counsel to people who need counsel, and they seem to be the answer to everyone's prayers, but they have been unable to get their own breakthrough.

I realize that dealing with life challenges is a part of the overall vision of God for His people. The overcomers have obstacles to overcome. In order to be "more than conquerors," as Paul wrote in Romans 8:37, there are battles that must be fought. Despite this, we should be partakers of the manifold promises of God! To experience this level of life, we must be good stewards of our *will*. We must *will* to be whole or to experience the full *soteria* or *salvation* of God.

Luke 18:30 (KJV) speaks of the "manifold more" that we can receive in life now and in the world to come. The word *manifold* refers to the many-faceted blessings of God. The flow of God's blessings can be compared to the manifold in a car. Everything comes from one source, which is through Jesus Christ. Through Him God's promises are distributed to every part of our lives (like the engine) to make them run smooth. This is why we need inner healing. When our spiritual engines break down, it affects every part of our lives.

Cars can be driven but run rough when something in the engine needs tuning up. Many Christians are barely making it in life and struggle every day. Yet, as I've already pointed out, Jesus came that we might have life and *that we have it more abundantly*. A soul that is running rough and struggling daily is not experiencing abundant life. To make the problem worse, many seek solutions in all the wrong places.

Make Jesus Christ Your Only Source

People are looking to many sources today for information about how to live their lives. But unless Jesus Christ is the source of the information we find, these sources are not a qualified path for a believer to walk upon. Even someone who has accomplished great things in the world and written a book about how to live life (for example, Oprah Winfrey) cannot show us the path to the abundant life available to us in Christ.

Believers who experience continual spiritual struggles need a spiritual tune-up. Inner healing is like a spiritual tune-up. A person can go through life with problems that they can never put their finger on. Some say it is like a dark cloud that rules over their heads. I have a chapter called "Putting Your Finger on the Enemy" in my book *Give It Back!* This topic is very serious to me. So many people live their lives feeling that something is following them around. They know something is not right, but they cannot put their finger on it. The only way to deal with subliminal matters such as this is to deal with the manifestations. Dark clouds and dark shadows always provoke manifestations. These manifestations must be identified and traced back to the roots.

Unless the Lord gives prophetic insight to these ghostly problems, dealing with them is like swinging at air. Paul said that he did not box like a person swinging at air and having no adversary. Though he knew there was a problem, he could not see it with the natural eye. So what was his solution? He buffeted his body and dealt with the manifestations. (See 1 Corinthians 9:26–27, NAS.) This meant that he dealt with how his body was responding to the unseen problem.

There was a young lady in my ministry who appeared to be very stable and mature. After getting to know her better, I found out that she sucked her thumb and needed to rub a fuzzy animal tail until she went to sleep. The attachment that she had to this habit was uncontrollable. Whenever she faced challenges in life, she would run into seclusion and suck her thumb and rub her animal tail for comfort. She said that it made her feel better. No one ever had the nerve to tell her that this was not godly behavior.

I knew she was acting out or manifesting something that was operating from behind the scenes. Not only did I tell her that this kind of action was not of the Lord, but I also told her that it was idolatrous and demonic! She was casting her cares on this behavior, and it had become her god. She was a very intelligent young lady, but she was dumbfounded when I told her simply to stop it! She said, "I have done this since I can remember. Every time my fuzzy tail gets too raggedy, my mom sends me a new one. I cannot just stop."

I told her that she had a choice to make. She could choose to be addicted to this soul tie, or she could move on. After nearly thirty years, for the first time in her life she chose to get rid of the object and to stop sucking her thumb. Immediately the habit was broken, and since then she has moved on in life.

This young lady admitted that she had never had a relationship with her mother, who is a crack addict. She had to grow up fast and was deprived of any real childhood. She spent her childhood taking care of her siblings while still a child herself. The sucking of the thumb and the rubbing of the fur were the manifestations of a part of her life that she missed—being a child. The root of the problem was rejection. She never received the attention that she needed as a little girl.

Just like an automobile, when man has an inner problem, there will be signs! I call these signs *manifestations*. We completed several deliverance sessions with the young lady mentioned above, but the signs were still there. We can keep changing the oil on a car (such as casting out devils) and filling it up with gas (getting people filled with the Holy Ghost), but if that car is still running rough, a mechanical diagnostic test must be done. Inner healing ministry is a spiritual diagnostic test that identifies the problem and fixes it.

Inner healing deals with the things that operate behind the scenes, which can cause heart trouble. Inner healing exposes and ministers to subliminal bondages that stop the flow of God in the lives of believers. The body of Christ needs inner healing ministers who, through the power of the Holy Ghost, will troubleshoot the manifestations in the lives of people and help them to get rid of the root problems in order to walk in victory. Inner healing ministry is for believers, not nonbelievers.

> **INNER HEALING MINISTRY IS A SPIRITUAL DIAGNOSTIC TEST THAT IDENTIFIES THE PROBLEM AND FIXES IT.**

The only way a person can be whole is to choose wholeness. The first step toward inner healing is to accept Jesus Christ as Lord *and* Savior. Many will accept Him as Savior and ignorantly deny His existence in their lives as Lord. The word *Lord* is *kurios*, and it means "supreme ruler and controller." Jesus does not come into our lives merely to keep us out of hell. He comes to give us abundant life in the earth realm. In order for this to occur, He must be Lord, or in total control.

When we give Jesus permission to control our lives, it enables us to make the right choices. Making the right choices in life is the maintenance schedule we follow to ensure that we will not break down. I have ministered to many people who have experienced nervous breakdowns. The source of every nervous breakdown has always been rooted in making wrong choices. This is true even if the individual's breakdown was the result of a tragedy over which they had no choice. No matter what we face in life, we must choose to give it to Jesus. The devil makes this seem so hard when, in fact, it is so simple.

A poignant example of how to give things to Jesus is found in the story of how the hymn *It Is Well With My Soul* was written. Horatio Spafford, his wife, and four daughters lived in Chicago just before the Great Chicago Fire. In the great fire of 1871, he lost all of his vast real estate investments. Two years after the fire he sent his four daughters and wife by ship to England, and the ship sank, killing all four girls. Spafford boarded the next ship to join his bereaved wife in England. While sailing across the same location where his daughters had perished, he penned the words, "When sorrows like sea billows roll,

63

whatever my lot, Thou hast taught me to say, 'It is well, it is well with my soul.'"[1] Out of this tragedy, this husband and wife who had lost their children became missionaries and started a ministry that later provided shelter to children who had no parents.[2]

> **MAKING THE RIGHT CHOICES IN LIFE IS THE MAINTENANCE SCHEDULE WE FOLLOW TO ENSURE THAT WE WILL NOT BREAK DOWN.**

In Luke 18:29 Jesus told His disciples that every man or woman who leaves house, parents, brothers, wife, or children for the kingdom of God will receive the *manifold more* promised by God in this present life or in the life to come. Horatio G. Spafford chose to give his losses to God and move on with kingdom business. How many would have cursed God and denied His existence after so much loss? Even when it seems as though life has not dealt a fair hand, it must be well with our soul. We must choose to live and move on.

Throughout the Bible, true leaders always put a demand on the people to make a choice. In the Old Testament, the Zadok priests taught the people the difference between right and wrong so that they could make the right choices. The Zadok priests were able to stand before the Lord and to minister to the people. (See Ezekiel 44:10–15.) The Levite priests had sinned against God. God said they were far away and went astray from Him through idolatry. God allowed these backslidden preachers to continue to minister in the sanctuary, but the curse was that they could not minister to Him. However, the Zadok priests were able to minister to the people and to the Lord, and they would keep the commandment of Leviticus 10:10. They taught the people the difference between what was holy and unholy.

On Mount Carmel, Elijah asked the people, "How long will you falter between two opinions?" (1 Kings 18:21). When the Israelites began to serve the idolatrous gods of their neighbors, Joshua told them, "Choose for yourselves this day whom you will serve" (Josh. 24:15).

When Moses returned to the camp and saw how Aaron had led the people into building a golden calf to worship, he stood in the entrance to the camp and said, "Whoever is on the LORD's side, come to me" (Exod. 32:26). In Deuteronomy 30:19, God told the children of Israel through Moses, "I have set before you life and death, blessing and cursing; therefore choose life, that both you and your descendants may live." Moses commanded that the people choose life so that they might live.

As we choose life, generational curses are broken off of our seed, and they receive the life that we chose also. We can affect our entire generation by the choices we make. It all starts with the individual decisions we make in life. Romans 12:2 says that we should not be conformed to the world but transformed by the renewing of our minds. Transformation requires change! When we make the right choices in life, it puts a demand on our souls to be changed.

The reciprocal effect of making right choices is that right choices come back to you. In other words, when you sow right choices, you will reap more right choices. Romans 12:2 also says that when your mind is renewed, you will be able to prove (for yourself) what the will of God is for your life. This means that when you give God your will, you get His will in return. This passage identifies the ingredients of God's will as "that good and acceptable and perfect will of God."

1. *The good will.* This is the *agathos* of the Lord. It refers to the benefits of the will of God that result from presenting obedience to God over sacrifice.

2. *The acceptable will.* This is the *euarestos* of the Lord. It is that which is well pleasing to the Lord and in full agreement with the Lord.

3. *The perfect will.* This is the *teleios* of the Lord, or that which is complete in labor, growth, and mental and moral character concerning the will of the Lord.

I believe these levels concerning the will of God are listed in order of progression. The *good will* is when we choose to obey the will of God, the *acceptable will* is when we actually learn to come in agreement with the will of God, and the *perfect will* is when we mature in moving in the will of God. I believe that as we submit our will to the pattern that God has laid out concerning His will, the perfect will of God can be achieved in our lives. The renewing of the mind is actually a type of renovation. The old must be torn down for the new to come. It is the same principle concerning the will of God. Just as our mindsets must be destroyed for us to receive the mind of Christ, so must our plans and purposes be destroyed to be replaced by His. There is a supernatural exchange that must occur. Jesus said, "Not My will, but God's will be done!"

TRANSFORMATION REQUIRES CHANGE!

If you are struggling with walking in abundant life, I have one question to ask: Will you be made whole? Will you allow a divine exchange to take place in your life? If you are not a believer, you must accept Jesus as Lord and Savior today. If you are a believer and are experiencing less than God has for you, I command you today to receive abundant life. The word *abundant* is *perissos,* and it means "to have excessive overflowing life." To have *perissos* means to have so much life that you have to share it with someone.

Salvation is supposed to flow out of us to touch others. When we settle for anything less than what God has for us, we not only cheat ourselves, but we also cheat those who are supposed to benefit from it. I cannot speak for anyone else, but I refuse to spend my life doing what God will allow me to get away with. To me, this is what the permissive will of God is about. It is when we give birth to an Ishmael because we are not strong enough to wait on Isaac. Today we are still fighting wars that began when Abraham settled for the permissive will of God.

I believe many Christians have struggles because they pursued the permissive will of God over His perfect will. The permissive will of God may be enough for you to get by, but it will never affect a generation for change. I challenge you to purpose to be whole and to experience all that salvation has for you.

chapter 6

THE INFLUENCE OF
RULING SPIRITS

E PHESIANS 2:1–2 REFERS to the prince of the power of the air that rules over the children of disobedience. The word *disobedience* is *apeitheia* in the Greek, and it means "to willfully refuse to obey or believe." This passage also mentions a habitual cycle and an influence that works on the inside of the person being ruled. This proves that a control is enforced from the second heaven that affects what is on the inside of a person in the earth realm.

Many do not understand that demons do not have to be on the inside of a person to control them; they just rule over them. Ephesians 6:12 speaks of "rulers of the darkness of this world" (KJV). Many people cast out demons, but they neglect to understand the importance of breaking the power of ruling spirits. This can be a great obstacle in the ministry of inner healing. Ruling powers must be broken from position over the heads of people.

THE CONNECTION TO INNER HEALING

Because of the influence mentioned in Ephesians 2:2, there is still a connection from the dark side to what is going on inside the person. Luke 11:35 warns that we not allow the light in us to be darkness. Darkness is always present in bondage. When a ruling spirit abides over a person's head, it is like an unseen prison that locks them down. This cannot be dealt with just by casting spirits out of these people. They must be disconnected from dark clouds that rule over their heads.

> **TRANSFORMATION IS A LIFETIME JOURNEY AND NOT A VACATION.**

Ruling spirits affect where a person is seated in the spirit. A person who habitually follows the course of the world cannot be seated in heavenly places with Christ Jesus. People are either seated in heavenly places with Jesus or directly connected with second-heaven activity. Where people are seated in the spirit realm determines which heaven rules over their head.

The place in the spirit where people are seated also determines how they think. There is a difference between being *worldly-minded* and *carnally minded*. Romans 12:2 refers to being worldly-minded when it tells us not to be conformed to the world but to be transformed by the renewing of our minds. Notice that the word *renewing* is used, not the word *renewal*. The renewing of the mind is a continual process. Transformation is a lifetime journey and not a vacation. It is a continual process. The Bible calls it an ever-increasing splendor that takes us from one degree of glory to another. (See 2 Corinthians 3:18, AMP.)

BEING WORLDLY-MINDED VS. BEING CARNALLY MINDED

Let's set the record straight. I do not believe that a person of the world can be worldly. They cannot be *worldly*, which means "to be like the world"—*they are the world!* It is like saying I am like Kimberly Daniels. No, I cannot be *like* her; I *am* Kimberly Daniels! So we are safe to say that a worldly-minded person is a person in the church who thinks like the world, keeping his or her mind on the things of the world.

A carnally minded person does not necessarily have to be worldly. An example of a carnally minded person is a very religious person who may not be bound by the things of the world. This person does not necessarily desire material things such as worldly music or the latest fads. On the other hand, the person may deny the true things of the Spirit of God.

The Bible declares that a carnal mind will always be at war against the things of God (Rom. 8:7). The word *carnal* is only mentioned in the New Testament. The Greek word is *sarx*, and it means the unregenerate fleshly mind. An example of a person being carnally minded but not worldly-minded is an old-fashioned churchwoman. This woman wears very modest clothing, no makeup, and avoids music and fellowship with the things and people of the world. She does not watch television or believe that Christians should be involved in professional athletics. On the other hand, she is bound by masturbation behind the scenes and is very jealous hearted and given to the spirit of hate. This woman is a gossiper and is always in disagreement with the leadership at her church. She is not worldly, but she definitely is carnal.

Carnality is the flesh as it was exposed to the soul and its human nature. These passions and frailties were exposed to Adam and Eve in the Garden of Eden. They were introduced to their inability to stand in the presence of God due to carnality. All of a sudden they were figuring things out for themselves. This is what carnality does. It wars against the things of the Spirit and leans toward the things of the natural with mere intellect (Rom. 8:6). This leads to death. Adam and Eve did not physically die for hundreds of years, but a spiritual death took place that gave birth to carnality, the enemy of God. Witches call carnally minded Christians "natural men" or saints who walk by sight rather than faith. The Hebrew word *naam* relates to the natural man. Its meaning is pleasure! Pleasure is the tendency that people have to walk by what pleases their flesh.

Adam and Eve could not have been worldly-minded because they were not yet exposed to the world. They were still in the garden. *Gan* is the Hebrew word for garden. It is defined as a "fenced-off area." The world was outside of that fenced area. The garden represented the presence of God or the place where Adam and Eve met God. Adam and Eve were forced to leave the garden because no flesh or carnality can glory in God's presence. When the Bible says that Adam and Eve knew they were "naked," this word *naked* comes from a Hebrew word *'aram*, which means to be made bare by becoming smooth, subtle, and crafty. This awareness of their nakedness put them under a new rule that caused them to take on the same spirit as that to which they had submitted themselves.

THE SPIRITUAL WARFARE OF INNER HEALING

Eve allowed the enemy to affect her atmosphere, and it changed her environment. I heard a teaching from Bishop Tudor Bismark that forever changed my life. He spoke of how a sustained atmosphere creates a climate. He explained that climates produce strongholds, and strongholds change the thinking of the people. We all know that as a man thinks, he is! (See Proverbs 23:7.) Strongholds not only change thinking, but they eventually change people.

On the flip side, to get caught up in the stronghold of God is the only way to be renewed in our minds. This principle that Bishop Bismark taught lined up with the revelation I received on ruling spirits. I related it to ministering inner healing to people who were held captive in their minds. We must do spiritual warfare over the minds of people who are bound in the strongholds of the enemy. Some ministers approach inner healing issues by immediately dealing with the individual. I have found that before you can ever deal with what is going on inside an individual, you must deal with atmospheres, environments, and strongholds that affect that person.

It is very important that intercessors are involved in the ministry process of inner healing. They do not have to be on the scene, but they need to be praying somewhere (before, during, and after the session). Though people may be in prison within themselves, the key to unlocking their liberty must open the door to the spirit realm first.

THE WEAPONS OF OUR WARFARE

Second Corinthians 10:4–5 is an important scripture to use for inner healing. I have dealt with people who could not receive healing because of rebellious thoughts, thus making the counseling process a nightmare experience. In many cases, people were so far gone it was impossible for me to reach them unless I broke the second heaven connection that ruled over their heads.

Let's take a look at the scripture:

> For the weapons of our warfare *are* not carnal but mighty in God for pulling down strongholds, casting down arguments and every high thing that exalts itself against the knowledge of God, bringing every thought into captivity to the obedience of Christ.

There are several points we must get out of this passage.

1. We cannot use carnality in warfare.

Remember that carnality is reason and intellect without the Holy Spirit. I am not saying that as ministers we cannot use our natural gifts and abilities. What I am saying is that they have to take second place to the Holy Spirit. We need research, education, and training. These

73

are support systems that lay a foundation, but the Holy Spirit must be our source.

Apostolic authority, the spirit of prophecy, discerning of spirits, and godly counsel are very important in the inner healing process. Apostolic authority is simply having authority to do what you are doing because you are a "sent one," and you did not just "up and go." Having the spirit of prophecy is the ability to flow and hear God to minister tailor-made counsel to an individual. The spirit of prophecy releases not only an accurate word but also a word in due season. Hitting or missing in the Spirit can damage a person and make that person's problems worse. The person receiving counseling will surely lose confidence.

Discerning of spirits is very important, because it gives the counselor the ability to know what is happening in the spirit realm. In the minds of many, discerning of spirits is mostly limited to seeing demons. This school of thought limits the true strength of the gift. Discerning of spirits is a Holy Ghost–given ability to peep into the spirit realm and know what time it is for real! It is very helpful to understand what is going on in the spirit realm despite what it looks like in the natural. The Bible says that what we see is temporal, and what we cannot see is eternal (2 Cor. 4:18). To help people, ministers must have an eye in the Spirit to see what they *cannot see* in the natural.

I have had cases with individuals who I felt were hopeless. They seemed to get worse by the minute. To my amazement, the worse the circumstances became, the closer the person came to his or her breakthrough. But because I received unction from the Holy Ghost and pressed through, the person was made whole.

Inner healing is a battle for the wholeness of a person. No two cases are the same. You can have two people with identical issues, and unless you troubleshoot each issue separately, you will lose ground in the Spirit. We may be sitting in nice comfortable rooms doing counseling sessions, but behind the scenes there is a war going on. The weapons of this war cannot be figured out with twelve steps. They are not naturally discerned! If we follow natural patterns, we will always find ourselves stuck, starting over, and making excuses. If we follow the pattern that God lays out in the Spirit, it always gives room to the creativity of God to make a way.

This is why godly counsel is so important. The counsel of God knows how to deal with the people He created. When walking in godly counsel, a good counselor will die to strong personal opinion. What the counselor thinks about issues is not more relevant than what God thinks! Psalm 1:1 references ungodly counsel. Ungodly counsel is any counsel outside of the counsel of God. Even "good counsel" is nothing in comparison to "God counsel."

2. We can do warfare by pulling down strongholds on behalf of others.

There is clearly a difference between those called to general intercession and those assigned to be prayer warriors. The church needs to get the revelation that we are an army. In an army there are different ranks of soldiers. God has anointed some to be on the front lines of battle to stand in the gap against darkness. In biblical times the armies built fortresses with the intent of keeping their enemies out. It also provided a place where they could live and be protected. The enemy also has fortresses or strongholds that keep God out of the lives of His people. In these strongholds, the minds of people are trapped in vicious cycles. Prayer warriors are anointed by God to go in through warfare prayer and penetrate places to dethrone ruling spirits so that the minds of captives can be set free.

3. Every individual has the responsibility of casting down evil imaginations that attack his or her own mind.

Once ruling spirits have been dethroned, the person in captivity will be able to see more clearly. The Bible says that if the gospel is hidden, it is hidden by the god of this world (2 Cor. 4:2–3). This ruling spirit of the world is called the *kosmokrator*. When this ruling spirit is dethroned from a person's life, that person is in a better place to receive counsel, and he or she can be responsible for casting down evil imaginations that attack his or her own mind.

4. Ministers must help individuals under attack to recognize the high things that exalt themselves against the knowledge of God (2 Cor. 10:4–6).

The phrase *high thing* in verse 5 is *hupsoma* in the Greek, and it is an elevated place or thing that creates a barrier in the minds of people. The word *itself* is *autos* in the Greek. It means to be trapped in one's own mind. The developmental disorder of autism is an interesting parallel to this spiritual principle. Children who suffer from autism have little or no ability to form social relationships because their minds seem to exist in a world of their own. Just so, the ruling spirit of this world entraps many into carnal strongholds in the mind, creating a barrier against the knowledge of God. Every disobedient thought that does not line up with the knowledge of Christ must be arrested and brought into the obedience of Christ. This takes the participation of the counselee and the counselor to identify and deal with every thought that breaks alignment with God's will.

THE PARABLE OF THE TREE

The alignment of God starts from the root system of a believer and lines up with their covering. In Psalm 1:3 believers are compared to trees planted by the rivers of water. I believe that we are like trees in the spirit realm. This is how we bear fruit. Bearing fruit is not optional for believers! God reminds us that He chose us and we did not choose Him. He also says He chose us that we may bear fruit and that our fruit would remain (John 15:16).

Jesus cursed the roots of the fig tree because it had no fruit. It only had leaves. (See Mark 11:13–14.) The Greek word for *leaves* is *phullon*, and it means "to sprout or to be a shoot off of the original." Jesus cursed the tree because there was no alignment with His root purpose. It was a diversion from the original plan of God. When God promises an Isaac, we do not have to create an Ishmael.

Judges 9:7–15 gives a parable about a group of trees. The trees were looking for a king to reign over them, and they considered the olive tree, fig tree, grapevine, and the bramble tree for the job. All of the trees responded differently to the request.

+ The olive tree did not want to leave its fatness to rule over the trees. This represented prosperity.

+ The fig tree did not want to leave its sweetness to rule over the trees. This represents that which is relished, satisfies, and brings comfort.

+ The grapevine did not want to leave its new wine to rule over the trees. This represented a new move of God.

+ The bramble tree told the trees, "If in good faith you are anointing me to rule over you, then take refuge in my shade; but if not, let fire come out of me and devour you."

The bramble tree did not make excuses but put a demand on the people to make a choice. The bramble tree represented how God rules over us. He demands us to make a choice. God took me to Deuteronomy 28 when I was first saved. I felt His welcome and love, but I also experienced the seriousness of His warnings to me to obey Him at any cost. Verses 1–14 teach on how we will experience the blessings of God if we obey Him. Verses 15–64 teach on the curses that will come if we do not line up with God's will. I will never forget thinking that there were so many more curses than blessings. It is true that the generational curses do not go back as far as the generational blessings go forward. (See Exodus 20:5–6.) But when I look at Deuteronomy 28, the repercussions are more when we willfully choose to disobey God!

In Judges 9:7 Jotham made the announcement about the selection of a king from Mount Gerizim. This is the mountain of the blessing where things were rocky and hard. Mount Ebal was the mountain of the curse where things were made smooth and easy. God commands us to put the blessings on one mountain and the curses on the other (Deut. 11:29). He demands separation!

Each of the first three trees in Judges 9 highlighted its *good* quality. This represented what would rule over the heads of the other trees (people) if that tree was chosen as ruler. It was a showboat of idolatry. The bramble tree put a demand on the people to make a choice. Bramble trees are in the rosebush family. Roses are beautiful, but if you handle them wrong, the thorns can hurt you. This is how it is with the Word of God—how we handle it will bless or curse us.

Some people live under the rule of the god of prosperity, some live under the rule of comfort, and others abide under the dominion of the latest move of God (through them). As believers we can take comfort, be prosperous, and experience legitimate moves of God by standing on 2 Corinthians 4:2. This scripture says that we should not handle the

Word of God in deceit. In good faith we can allow the Word of God to rule over our lives as we take refuge in Jesus.

It is the nature of man to be ruled over. We were created to live under the influence of the almighty God. People, places, and things infiltrate that space that was created for God to rule over us as His creation. As a result of this, things get out of order in our lives.

Do you feel that ruling spirits need to be broken off of your life? Does the order of God need to be restored so that you may receive deep inner healing? Let the process begin by praying this prayer:

PRAYER TO BREAK THE POWER OF RULING SPIRITS

Father God, in the name of Jesus I renounce the powers of the rulers of the darkness of this world. I renounce spirits of rebellion, carelessness, and unbelief that may connect second-heaven activity to my life. I am a child of the King, an heir of God, and a joint heir with Christ. I am seated in heavenly places with Jesus. I draw from the anointing of the mercy of God, and I am not discouraged, spiritless, and despondent. I am encouraged, responding to the will of God, and full of life. I have renounced every high thing that attempts to exalt itself against the knowledge of God. I will not be put in seclusion by the enemy through pride, deception, and being hidden in bondage. I refuse to deal craftily or practice trickery or treachery when it comes to the Word of God. I renounce adulteration or mishandling of the truth in a dishonest manner. I will deal in life and with things concerning the Word of God openly and candidly. My conscience is clear, and I am in total alignment with the Word and the will of God. I am a tree planted by the rivers of water. My root system is strong, and the flow of God is consistent in my life. Jesus is the author and finisher of my faith, and His lordship rules over every area of my life. The powers of ruling spirits are broken off of me forever; I open my heart to healing in my innermost parts. Amen.

chapter 7

STRONG IN THE LORD
(PART I)

S HORTLY AFTER THE death of Moses, God had a conversation with his successor, Joshua. In His words to Joshua, God emphasized, "*Only you* be strong and courageous." God wanted Joshua to make it personal. No one else could be strong and of good courage for him. In Joshua 1:7–8 we can read the instructions that God gave to Joshua:

> Only you be strong and very courageous, that you may do according to all the law which Moses My servant commanded you. Turn not from it to the right hand or to the left, that you may prosper wherever you go. This Book of the Law shall not depart out of your mouth, but you shall meditate on it day and night, that you may observe and do according to all that is written in it. For then you shall make your way prosperous, and then you shall deal wisely and have good success.
> —Joshua 1:7–8, AMP

Let's take a look at the true meaning of the words *strong* and *courage* in the Hebrew tongue.

STRONG

This word is *chazaq* in Hebrew. It means to:

+ Seize—Nothing in God will come easy, it must be taken by force.

+ Cure—The strength of God on the inside of His people anoints us to heal.

+ Help—We are only strong in the Lord when it assists others around us.

+ Repair—The people of God are restorers and repairers of the things darkness has torn down.

+ Fortify—The camps of God were always strengthened by strong walls. No fortification signifies weakness and gives the enemy access.

+ Restrain—The army of the Lord is called to bind and loose. The will of God cannot be loosed into the earth realm until God's people take their rightful positions and restrain that which comes against it.

+ Conquer—Joshua was ordained to conquer. So is every born-again believer.

+ Confirm—Nothing can be fulfilled without the confirmation of the Lord.

+ Be constant—The blessings of God require consistency. God is not a "wham, bam, thank you, ma'am" one-night-stand God.

- Take courage—Courage is not given to anyone. It must be taken! We take courage when we overcome fear and obey the Lord no matter what it costs.

- Be established—A sure foundation is a blessed assurance.

- Make hard—Life in God does not make us soft but hard. Iron really does sharpen iron.

- Maintain—The saints must inspect, keep, and hold on to the things of God. They are precious and cannot be taken for granted!

- Play the man—The born-again believer is *all that!* The greater One is on the inside of us, and we can do all things through Christ Jesus who strengthens us (Phil. 4:13). As long as we remain humble and submitted unto God, it is all right to "play the man," God's man, whom He takes joy in seeing walk in dominion!

- Wax mighty—To wax mighty means to go from something small and insignificant to a great and awesome thing in the earth realm. When we wax mighty, only God can get the glory.

- Prevail—The Lord has given us dominion in the earth to put His enemies to open shame. Our lives must prove to be superior in strength, power, and influence over the heathen nations. As we dominate and have greater influence, they become jealous. This is the plan of God—to use us to make the world jealous (Rom. 11:14).

+ Be recovered—The fact that God demands us to recover denotes the fact that we are called to go through some things. The key to "going through" in God is being like a Timex watch (take a licking and keep right on ticking).

+ Strengthen self—There can be no courage without encouragement. Sometimes encouragement will be far away when we are under attack. Like David, the people of God must know how to encourage themselves in the Lord (1 Sam. 30:6, KJV).

+ Be stout—To be stout means to be "fat" or to prosper. It is no secret that it is the will of God for us to prosper in every area of our lives.

+ Be sure—Confidence in Him is like a healing balm to a wound.

+ Take hold—God wants us to have sharp discernment concerning what is ours. Grab hold of it, and hold on to it with a bulldog grip.

+ Behave self-valiantly—God has also called every individual believer to be brave and stouthearted. We must be mighty men and women of valor. To be people of valor means to walk in boldness and determination despite hardship. To walk in valor also means to walk in our ultimate worth or value. When we walk in less than what God has called us to walk in, it depreciates our value. The curse of this is that we can never obtain the excellence that God has called us to.

✦ Withstand—The Bible says that we must resist the devil and he will flee (James 4:7). To *withstand* means to successfully resist and oppose in opposition. There is no victory in God without conflict.

There are other Hebrew words that relate to being strong, such as:

- *Chazeq*—This means to wax louder. Our voices must cry loud in the wilderness and on the mountaintops.

- *Chozeq*—This means to have strength and power.

- *Chezqah*—This means to have power that prevails and is raised above all the rest. We do not just have power; we have *the power*.

- *Chozqah*—This means to have vehement force. Vehement force is hostile, zealous, and violent. We are the violent, and we take by vehement force.

COURAGEOUS

Two of the Hebrew words for courage are *chazaq* and *amats*. Both of these words relate to strength. *Amats* literally means to be of strong color. *Strong's Exhaustive Concordance* relates it to the color red. The color yellow has been traditionally related to being a coward. God has not called us to be yellow in the Spirit. Red represents fire! When we are on fire for the Lord, we have great courage; this is the remedy for discouragement. It is hard to be "dis-couraged" when you are full of courage!

> **MANY PEOPLE NEED TO BE HEALED FROM *INNER WEAKNESSES*.**

From my review of these terms and their definitions, I believe it would be safe for me to give an interpretation of Joshua 1:7–8 that will help people who are struggling with weaknesses in their lives. Let me start by saying that everyone has a weakness! The strongest man ever recorded, Samson, had a weakness that Delilah used against him. Paul had a thorn in his side, which if we were to interpret it would indicate a secret weakness. So it is not a sin to have a weakness. The trouble comes in when we are overcome by our weaknesses. This is my version of Joshua 1:7–8:

> Remember that you cannot be weak and walk in fear. Walking without fear is the only way you will be able to obey Me. Do not allow your weaknesses and insecurities to blow you to and fro. Be stable and steadfast in Me. Continue to study, meditate on, and confess My Word all the time so that you will line up with it. If you will be faithful to these things, you will be prosperous, walk in divine wisdom, and never fail.

Many people need to be healed from *inner weaknesses*. They suffer from weaknesses and fears and do not realize that these things stem from hidden bondages. Let's review the sources of these bondages.

THE SOURCES OF HIDDEN BONDAGE

Suppression

Suppression is one of the hardest sources of bondage I have dealt with. It is the willful or unconscious pressing down of things below the level of consciousness. Dealing with this kind of bondage takes a prophetic gifting because it can often go undetected. When a person pushes things deep down on the inside, it is like putting trash in a trash compactor. Though it is formed into a nice, neat, little package at the bottom of the container, it is still there and will eventually begin to stink. Foul, unclean spirits of suppression lie dormant in the lives of people for years. Suppression is:

+ That which is withheld from disclosure or publication to bring forth evidence or truth

+ A spirit of arrested development that denies any growth

+ That which is subdued as a result of revolt or rebellion against the laws of God

+ Cruelty that crushes the emotions and reduces the flow of God in a person's life to make it rocky and filled with blockages

+ That which breeds a false strength and causes a demonic coping to hide the true inner weakness of the person

+ Rooted in pride and rebellion and falls under the order of the "great transgression" (subliminal bondage) spoken of in Psalm 19:13

Suppression manifests itself in the lives of people when they least expect it. Below are examples of bondages that result due to suppression:

+ A child who has been obedient in the home starts college and becomes extremely rebellious. Every rule that child could not break at home, he or she begins to break while in college. Whenever mom and dad did not allow that child to have his or her own way at home, the disobedient spirit was suppressed. This suppression eventually came to the surface when the child left home.

+ During most of his childhood, a young man was molested by his stepfather. He never shared this situation with anyone. The experience was so traumatic that he pushed it to the back of his mind, as though it never happened. Later in life he became very successful, and a male business partner approached him in a homosexual manner. The young man was lured into a homosexual relationship as a result. He never received a release from this situation, and the spirit of this suppression hid behind his personality.

+ A little girl lost her mother at an early age. She never really had a healthy mourning period. People marveled at her ability to cope and adjust to the death of her mother so smoothly. She never had another female in her life to be a mother figure from that time forth. This little girl grew up to be a multimillionaire and became the CEO of one of the largest corporations in the world. Her corporation has a large turnover for females in the company. The little girl, now CEO, has always kept barriers up in her life and cannot have fruitful relationships with any women.

All of the instances noted above are cases of what I call *early life suppression*, which eventually surfaced due to *timed-release curses*. A *timed-release curse* is a curse that has a right to abide in a person's life because of a hook in the soul. This hook in the soul, which is the actual incident that causes the suppression, has a right to come out of hiding as a result of an omen or prognostication of a demonic appointment. The strongman of the spirit of suppression is a demon called *Father Time*. Father Time has a stopwatch to assure that the timed-release curse is ignited in the demonic time set. When people suppress things in their lives, they appear to have victory in an area of their lives until Father Time says. "Time is up—the suppression must manifest itself now!"

WHETHER IT IS EMOTIONAL, MENTAL, OR DEMONIC SUPPRESSION, THE HOOK MUST BE REMOVED SO THAT THE DEVIL CAN HAVE NO PART IN US.

My husband has a friend with whom he used to get high in a crack house. This friend had a successful business in a major city and was doing very well. Though he was not using drugs anymore, he was not saved, and his conversation showed that his mind was not renewed. One day as I was praying for him, I saw Father Time sitting on his chest and holding a stopwatch. I warned him that the enemy was coming to pull him back into the drug scene. I described what I saw sitting on his chest. He did not take me seriously, and within a year he was back on crack. He has lost his family, job, home, and all that he had acquired. As far as we know, he is still on drugs. This man calls my husband from time to time and always mentions the little man that I saw sitting on his chest.

The moral of this story is that just because people stop doing an act does not mean they are delivered. Just as emotions can be suppressed, so too can demons be suppressed. Demons can lie dormant and be activated by Father Time. Whether it is emotional, mental, or demonic suppression, the hook must be removed so that the devil can have no part in us. When the devil has no part in us, it breaks the stopwatch of Father Time.

Oppression

Oppression is a harsh burdensome weight of heaviness on the mind of a person that results in tormenting spirits of cruelty. The strongman of oppression is the taskmaster. Though the root of the bondage is inside the person, the taskmaster rules over his or her head in tyranny. Oppressed persons tend to have no ability to function under the circumstances of the bondage. They usually live with manifestations they cannot put their finger on. They do things they cannot explain and often find themselves in predicaments that make them operate outside of their normal personalities. The spirit of the slave is upon them because they have no authority or rule over their spirit. The strength of natural and spiritual slavery is the spirit of heaviness. It weighs the oppressed person down under a load on his or her back.

I have seen many be delivered from spirits of infirmity in their backs. When we prayed and removed the load of the taskmaster from their backs, they received healing in their bodies. Many people have physical back ailments as a result of a spirit of oppression. When dealing with heaviness and oppression, the yoke must be destroyed. A *yoke* is an object that connects people to reins that guide their lives. The reins of the yoke must be broken and destroyed. This can only take place by the anointing.

> And it shall come to pass in that day, that his burden shall be taken away from off thy shoulder, and his yoke from off thy neck, and the yoke shall be destroyed because of the anointing.
> —Isaiah 10:27, KJV

The word *yoke* is `ol` in Hebrew, and it refers to that which is imposed upon the neck. The neck is the place of bondage. I do not think that it is a coincidence that Leviathan's (the king of pride) strength is in his neck. (See Job 41:1–22.) Oppressive spirits often yoke themselves with spirits of pride and deception to keep a person under the rule of the taskmaster without being aware of it.

chapter 8

STRONG IN THE LORD
(PART II)

I
N THIS CHAPTER I would like to teach on the threefold cord
of the sources of hidden bondage—obsession, depression,
and possession. These three bondages usually relate to each
other in some manner. They all hinder believers from being strong
in the Lord.

OBSESSION

Obsession is defined as the domination and preoccupation of the mind.
It causes a persistent troubling or besetting that hijacks the thoughts,
feelings, and eventually the will of a person. Obsession is connected
to a spirit of distraction, which does not allow the person to function
normally in life. The strongman of obsession is the spirit of addiction.

An obsessed person becomes an addict in regard to whatever has
besieged his or her mind. The addiction takes the person out of alignment with the will of God. Because of being out of place, the person
dwells in places that promote fear, anxiety, and error. The spirit of error
is not rooted in *what a person does* but in *where a person's mind abides*.
Error born out of obsession is a place in the spirit where the person
could not do right if he or she wanted to. People who are bound by
addictions such as crack, pornography, and gambling live in the realm
of obsession. The root of the problem is not the act but the fact that

their minds have been hijacked, and wherever the mind is, the body will follow.

The solution for any obsession is renewal of the mind. This can only happen by an encounter with Jesus Christ. The person must be delivered from the mental anguish that causes him or her to abide in the *place of the addiction.* He or she must literally get on another road in the spirit where deliverance is inevitable. When the person moves from the place of the addiction, the acts will cease.

Recently a young man in my ministry was supernaturally delivered from a lifestyle of drug dealing and street life. I have ministered to many young men in this situation, but something about his conversion really stood out. He went from night to day! Like my husband and me, he came on the Lord's side with full force. He walked into God and left thousands of dollars behind without a second thought. He had no means of support for his family, but he immediately learned how to trust God. I have not seen many cases like his, and I asked my husband what made his situation so different. He responded that this young man had been hit by a bolt of lightning. I agreed!

That's it—he had a Damascus road experience! This is the only way to come out of an obsessive bondage. Saul was obsessed with killing believers, and Jesus struck him down off his high horse. Saul went from killing believers to being killed as a believer. Obsessive bondage captures the minds of its victims. As extreme as it is, the only way to truly be delivered from obsessive addiction is for the mind to be hijacked by the Holy Ghost.

> **THE SOLUTION FOR ANY OBSESSION IS RENEWAL OF THE MIND.**

DEPRESSION

Depression is caused by a strong spirit of heaviness. The Hebrew word for *heaviness* is *keheh*, and it means to weaken the spirit. It also means to make dim like heavy smoke. Depression causes a person to be bent over in the spirit so they cannot see their way. The victim of depression walks under a dark cloud and has no joy. Depression makes a person sad, gloomy, and low in spirit. The end result of depression is no sensitivity to God because of dullness of heart. Another word for depression is *dispirited*. To be dispirited means to have no spiritual source to the point of being bound by the rule of the flesh. A depressed person cannot hear God while the intercom of the flesh is loud and clear. David asked God to enlighten his eyes or he would sleep the sleep of death (Ps. 13:3).

Depression is the number-one cause of suicide. Suicide is rooted in hopelessness and helplessness. People believe that there is no hope or help, and they sleep their lives away. I can remember at one time in my life when I was depressed. I was not saved and was at the lowest point in my life. I was tricked to believe that suicide was an option, and I contemplated it several times. The only thing that kept me alive was the fact that I had a little boy. I did not want him to live the rest of his life knowing that his mother committed suicide. I remember going to bed at night wishing that I would not wake up. I dreaded when the light of morning came.

I made it out of this dark situation and went into the military. In the military I met Jesus, and depression and suicide were no longer options for me. Though I did not meet Jesus immediately, God allowed me to get in a new environment that provided hope. This kept me until I was saved. Now that I am saved, I have vowed not to be depressed by devils but to depress devils. I have declared that my enemies shall have no rest. To everything that the dark side had released against me, I have sent a boomerang from the Lord back at them.

The first step in being healed of depression is *getting up*! Refuse to sleep the sleep of death! Ask the Lord to make your eyes light and allow you to see your way until you get your full deliverance. A little bit of deliverance is better than none. In other words, there is deliverance in simply getting up! A righteous man will fall down seven times but can rise again (Prov. 24:16). Most people do not die on their feet. You must lie down to die. If you are going through depression, stop right now and tell the devil, "I will not lie down and die!"

Once a person rises from the bed of depression with the Lord on his or her side, God Himself will displace the devils of heaviness. According to Isaiah 61:3, beauty will replace ashes, the oil of joy will replace mourning, and the garment of praise will displace the spirit of heaviness. There is deliverance for those who mourn in Zion.

If you do not know Jesus Christ as your Lord and Savior, accept Him in your heart now. Without the intervention of God in your life, there will always be depression and despair. There is only one way to combat depression—through the Word of God. A person who has been bowed down by the lies of depression can be lifted up by the truth of the gospel. Proverbs 12:25 says that heaviness of the heart makes a man stoop, but a good word makes him glad. In Psalm 119:28, the psalmist asked to be raised up and strengthened according to the promises of the Word of God.

I would especially like to encourage the men and women of God who have wrestled with depression. In Romans 9:2, Paul shared the fact that he was depressed. He said that he had bitter grief and continual sorrow of heart. In 2 Corinthians 2:1–2, Paul told the Corinthians that he would not come to them in heaviness and depression. He made it clear that he did not want to release the spirit of depression on those to whom he ministered or those who would be able to minister to him. It is clear that we need each other as ministers in the body of Christ. Whether you are a minister, a believer, a backslider, or a heathen, take a moment and get your heart right with God. Then pray this prayer with me:

> *I bind the spirit of heaviness in the name of Jesus! I command every false covering that would make my mind weary and the spirit despondent to go in Jesus's name. I break the curse of the "sleep of death" and decree that in my darkest nights I have hope that joy is coming in the morning. I command the sun to be my friend and not my enemy. I will rise up and let the enemies of my soul be displaced...forever! Every devil of heaviness, suicide, give up, and can't take it anymore—you lie down and die! I will live and not die. The walking dead is sent back to the caverns of hell to be tormented. You have failed your assignment. It is legal and official—YOUR ASSIGNMENT OF DEPRESSION AND HEAVINESS IS BROKEN FOREVER. Amen.*

In conclusion, I want to remind you that depression is a sin. We are commanded to walk in the joy of the Lord...it is our strength. Many are weak and despondent because they have allowed the enemy to steal their joy. You have been through your night season, but I declare that joy is coming in the morning. Rise up, receive it, and sin no more!

THERE IS ONLY ONE WAY TO COMBAT DEPRESSION—THROUGH THE WORD OF GOD.

Possession

Possession is one of my favorite topics to teach. So many people avoid it. The definition of *possession* is when a person is controlled to the point of seizure and ownership. A possessed person has been seized in his or her mind and body. There is deliverance for the possessed. The Bible has many examples of people who were possessed with devils and who received total deliverance:

+ The man in the tombs (Mark 5:1–14)

+ Mary Magdalene (Mark 16:9)

+ The damsel possessed with the python spirit in the Book of Acts (Acts 16:16–18)

In every one of these cases, the possessed person received supernatural deliverance from devils. Possessions were often related to people with infirmities like the epileptic and the paralytic. Whether it was control of the mind or infirmity of the body, the cure for demonic possession was faith in the power of Christ with prayer.

As I am writing this chapter, I can testify of the deliverance from possession of a crippled young boy who was in one of my services. He was carried up the stairs of our church in a wheelchair. His frail body sank down in the chair as I preached a very long message. I ministered on the supernatural that night, and the atmosphere was ignited with faith. It was a Wednesday night Bible study, yet the Lord unusually called an altar call for healing. The boy was rolled to the front of the church in his wheelchair. All of his limbs appeared to be weak and twisted. I called the demon out of the boy, and his mouth opened as wide as I had ever seen a human mouth open. His face began to distort, and his eyes poked out of his head. A demon came out of him!

When I grabbed his twisted arms, they straightened out before my eyes. When we stood him up, another demon came out of him. His legs stiffened, and he walked out of the wheelchair. He pushed the chair out of the church. The boy's family stated that he had not eaten in six weeks. He looked over at his mother and told her he was hungry. We are counseling with the family daily, and he is still walking and eating.

The million-dollar question is: "Can a Christian be possessed with a devil?" Absolutely! A Christian is more apt to be possessed than a regular person because of the revolving door of religion. People who play with God can be possessed with devils. Many believers use altar calls as a crutch, and it is very dangerous. They live sinful lives Monday through Saturday and come to church for a spiritual fix every Sunday. By Monday they are back in Jezebel's bed again. Matthew 12:44 warns us about the revolving door of religion when it comes to deliverance. Everything from which we have been delivered waits for a door to open to come back in.

The Bible says that the state of a man who swept his life clean but failed to block access back into his life was repossessed with the same demon and seven more (Matt. 12:43–45)! This passage continues by describing a wicked generation who, like the man in this passage, is seven times worse than at first. I believe this verse characterizes the wickedness in our world today. Surely this is the pattern that leads to possession.

PEOPLE WHO PLAY WITH GOD CAN BE POSSESSED WITH DEVILS.

Hebrews 6:4–6 describes a pattern of falling away after you have been enlightened with heavenly gifts and have tasted the good Word of

God, likening it to playing dice with your soul. If a Christian could not be possessed, there would be no apostasy. Apostasy is the great falling away spoken of in 2 Thessalonians 2:3 (AMP):

> Let no one deceive or beguile you in any way, for that day will not come except the apostasy comes first [unless the predicted great falling away of those who have professed to be Christians has come], and the man of lawlessness (sin) is revealed, who is the son of doom (of perdition).

The greatest example of a Christian being possessed with devils, in my opinion, is the fall of Carlton Pearson. He was once one of the most respected ministers in the body of Christ. No one could fathom that a man of his spiritual stature would put Jesus on the same level as the Baals of this land. He has taught that Jesus is the way...but not the only way. He also teaches that homosexuals are going to heaven, there is no hell, and the devil will be saved. Truly these are doctrines of devils. To preach messages of this sort, a person would have to be filled with Legion.

This new ministry of his, called *Inclusion*, only supports what I have been teaching for years. If a believer crosses the line into the land of *Nod*, he or she can not only be possessed with devils, but will also be trapped into the bottomless pit of reprobation. Now many of Dr. Pearson's associates support ministries that accept same-sex marriages, gay churches, and laws that are demonically initiated to shut the mouths of the preachers in the church.

Ecclesiastes 10:8 (KJV) states:

> Whoso breaketh a hedge, a serpent shall bite him.

No, the devil cannot cross the bloodline, but we can! If we choose to tempt God and play with the Holy Ghost, we will be bitten by the serpent *nachash*. This serpent strikes with interest, and the real poison of the bite will linger in your soul, lying in wait for the right moment, when it will manifest the results of the purpose for which it bit.

chapter 9

THE NAMES OF GOD

MANY PEOPLE ARE not able to encounter the Lord's love because they have wounded and bound souls. Inner healing goes to the root cause of many symptoms. It is by the Holy Spirit's power that we are able to connect with the cause of emotional torment. All healing requires being open to God and to the way He chooses to move in the healing process. Most of life's problems are due to some damaging dialogue or adverse actions that occurred in the past. Inner healing can be a deep experience when we get real.

We must also know who we are. All spiritual healing is contingent upon how much we are willing to see ourselves in light of the truth. This is often difficult because the truth hurts. Real healing is the correction of the soul. To have this, it is essential to recognize who God is intimately as the Creator of our soul. In order to know Him, we must learn to embrace Him by name.

THE FUNCTIONAL POWER OF A NAME

At the end of this chapter I have listed the names of God in Hebrew and Aramaic. The name of Jesus is the name above all names. Without a revelation, many call on that name in times of trouble. Some even ignorantly use His name in vain. The true essence of God is manifested through His many names. The names of God relate to the healing process of the whole man.

First, we must know the importance of names within the biblical context. One of the ways we can learn spiritual truths is from the Hebrew language itself. It is critical that we understand that there is more to a name than what most know or believe. Names are very significant in the Bible. Hebrew is not a language of description by appearance like most modern languages.

> **REAL HEALING IS THE CORRECTION OF THE SOUL.**

In the Hebrew language, names carry two things:

1. Character
2. Function

A name actually represented the actual character or nature of a person, place, or thing. Hebrew is descriptively functional, and the language actually lives. To understand this principle, let's look at Exodus 34:14 (KJV):

> For thou shall worship no other god: for the LORD, whose name is Jealous, is a jealous God.

This passage clearly presents the fact that God's name is not just *Jealous*—He *is* jealous! He is not just called by this name, but His very essence manifests the meaning of that name:

Jealous (definitions)

- Apprehensive of losing affection or position in one's life

- Intolerant of infidelity, disloyalty, or rivalry

+ Troubled by unfaithfulness

+ Solicitous or vigilant in maintaining or guarding what He considers His

+ Zeal that breeds much attention

These things do not list *how* God is but *who* God is. *He is jealous.*

In biblical times, God's people were not concerned with the appearance of a thing but how it functioned. In modern society, names are used for identification. Throughout the Old Testament we see how people named people, places, and things based on what happened. The first place where this occurs in the Bible is with Adam.

> And out of the ground the Lord God formed every [wild] beast and living creature of the field and every bird of the air and brought them to Adam to see what he would call them; and whatever Adam called every living creature, that was its name. And Adam gave names to all the livestock and to the birds of the air and to every [wild] beast of the field.
>
> —Genesis 2:19–20, AMP

After the Creation, God allowed Adam to name every living creature, livestock, and bird. The giving of the names to the animals was Adam's first observed act of obedience. It was one of the most important assignments Adam was given, because it represented dominion over creation. When Adam named the beasts and birds, he saw as God saw and was able to see the function of every animal.

Let's take a look at Genesis 22:13–14:

> Then Abraham lifted his eyes and looked, and there behind him was a ram caught in a thicket by its horns. So Abraham went and took the ram, and offered it up for a burnt offering instead of his

son. And Abraham called the name of the place, The-Lord-Will-Provide; as it is said to this day, "In the Mount of The Lord it shall be provided."

This passage shows the function of the Lord providing the sacrifice; therefore Abraham calls the place "Jehovah-jireh" (KJV). The term "it shall be provided" literally means, "be seen." This is one example of how Hebrew lives, as actually manifesting and not just as descriptive appearance. Something happened and showed the faithfulness of who the Lord is. His provision is a place for His purpose. The names of God throughout Scripture will demonstrate God's ability to manifest His will into the earth.

Often I have dealt with people who are bound as a result of a lack of identity. When we do not have a revelation of God and the true essence of His name, we fail to know our purpose. When we don't have a solid revelation of our purpose, we will lack the ability to function according to the plan of God. When we are not being who we were created to be, it then becomes difficult to live in divine wholeness. Spiritual wholeness can be easily attained through having a revelation of the names of God. Everything we need is in His name, which is His nature. Just as Adam named the animals in the second chapter of Genesis, so God reveals His nature to heal and His character to transform through His names. For those who call upon Him by name, there is a place we walk as sons and daughters.

El Nosei (the God Who Forgives)

> You answered them, O Lord our God;
> You were to them God-Who-Forgives,
> Though You took vengeance on their deeds.
>
> —Psalm 99:8

El Nosei is "the God Who Forgives." Forgiveness is the key to all healing. God's healing comes through His love and forgiveness. Our salvation from sin and death is premised on forgiveness.

> In Him we have redemption through His blood, the forgiveness of sins, according to the riches of His grace which He made to abound toward us in all wisdom and prudence.
> —Ephesians 1:7–8

Forgiveness is releasing the feeling of victimization. Over the years I have dealt with many people who walk in the *curse of the victim*. This is a curse whereby people take the position of the victim and are doomed never to experience victory in Jesus. There can be no victory from the position of the victim. When a person is in the position of the victim, they can never forgive. Unforgiveness is a cloud that overshadows a person and causes repeated cycles or patterns of negativity. When we cannot let things go and we remain in unforgiveness, we close the doors to the blessings of *El Nosei*, "the God Who Forgives."

The Bible makes it clear that if we do not forgive, we cannot be forgiven. Forgiveness is a requirement for healing to take place. Oh, what a blessing to dwell in the land of the forgiven. Deep inner healing changes our position in the spirit. When our position is changed, we have an opportunity to be changed. There can be no change if a person remains where they are:

+ The children of Israel had to move forward.

+ The lepers at the gate of Samaria had to move toward the enemy's camp.

+ The man at the pool of Bethesda had to take up his bed and walk.

Forgiveness changes our position and opens the doors of healing. Forgiveness is a healing balm to our souls. The healing balm of forgiveness causes peace of mind. Unforgiveness is rooted in a spirit of torment. Whenever there is torment, fear is hiding in the corridors.

> There is no fear in love; but perfect love casts out fear, because fear involves torment. But he who fears has not been made perfect in love.
>
> —I John 4:18

The forgiveness of *El Nosei* is rooted in perfect love. God has not given us a spirit of fear but of power, *love*, and a sound mind (2 Tim. 1:7). People who do not know the forgiveness of God can never imagine His love. The love of God releases a peace that surpasses all natural understanding. This is the only way a person can have a sound mind. The opposite of a sound mind is a tormented mind.

The Greek word for *torment* is *kolasis*, and it means to punish or hold as an offender. This is the exact opposite of the word *forgiveness*, which means to release or dismiss from the sentence. *El Nosei* is the *Father of pardons.* He has jurisdiction to release you from a spiritual death row or a dreadful life sentence.

Recently I was reading a letter from one of my relatives who is doing a life sentence in prison. He has accepted Jesus as his Lord and Savior, but the hardest thing for him to imagine is the forgiveness of God. He is in prison for murder. He asked, "Do you think the Lord will give me another chance?"

My response was easy: "Another chance is what forgiveness is all about."

Matthew 18:21 makes it real plain:

> Then Peter came to Him and said, "Lord, how often shall my brother sin against me, and I forgive him? Up to seven times?" Jesus said to him, "I do not say to you, up to seven times, but up to seventy times seven."

This passage proves several things. First, it lets us know that to be forgiven we must forgive. Then, it supports my earlier statement, "Forgiveness is all about another chance." When we do not receive the forgiveness of God in our lives, we are open to the tormentors. This ultimately takes us into a spirit of unforgiveness. It is one thing to have a one-time experience with unforgiveness but another to dwell in the spirit of it. The end result is that we close heaven over our lives.

Let's look at Matthew 5:25:

> Agree with your adversary quickly, while you are on the way with him, lest your adversary deliver you to the judge, the judge hand you over to the officer, and you are thrown into prison.

I know you are thinking, "What does this have to do with forgiveness?" Receive the revelation…

The adversary is the devil. He always does his job as usual. He comes to steal, kill, and destroy. Everything in the world has to line up with God whether it agrees to or not. The devil is doing what the Bible says he is supposed to do. The world is doing what it is supposed to do, but the problem comes when the saints do not do what they are supposed to do! When we agree with our adversary, we must line up with the Word of God. The Bible says that the enemy will come in like a flood, and we have to get in place for God to raise the standard. When cancer, divorce, and any other demonic assignment come, we must do our part—stand on the Word! The worst thing we can do while we are under attack is to cry like a baby, asking God, "Why?" You should already know why!

The kingdom of God suffers violence, and we must learn to *take it by force!* Doing so has a twofold meaning:

1. We take what is ours (by force) no matter what the enemy brings our way.

2. We take it! (Remember, be like Timex—take a licking and keep on ticking.)

Weapons form, but they will not prosper. We must learn to take the forming of a weapon and laugh in the devil's face while it does not prosper. This surely gives hell a headache. The devil sends his best bomb at us, yet when the smoke settles, we are rolling on the ground laughing at him. Every arrow from the devil is an opportunity for God to show up and show out! The enemy may send you a foreclosure notice or an AIDS report. Your job is to confess what the Word of God says concerning this situation and stand to see the salvation of the Lord.

After you have stood, the Bible says that the devil must flee. He has to take his lies and his symptoms with him. I know that the devil is not a little red man with a pointed tail, but I always visualize him running with his tail under his behind. Why? Because he is an unforgiven foe. There is no forgiveness for him. He is doomed and can never receive the redeeming love of *El Nosei*.

The devil is a hater, and he plots against us because he is jealous. His jealousy is rooted in the fact that we mess up so many times, and yet the Father is faithful to forgive us. He messed up one time, and that was "all she wrote"!

I pray that you receive the forgiveness of *El Nosei* right now. Do not allow the enemy to pull you into his place of eternal unforgiveness. The devil cannot forgive because he is an eternally damned unforgiven being.

John 10:5 warns us not to follow strange voices. The word *follow* is very important in this passage. It literally means, "to become one with" or "to get on the same road with." Do not follow the voice that would have you to walk in unforgiveness or reject the forgiveness of the Father. Get off that road!

***

Matthew 5:25 says that if we do not agree with our adversary (by standing on the Word), we will be turned over to a judge (critical spirit, Greek: *krites*). In doing this, we can very easily begin to judge our own situations and be turned over to the jailer, a spirit of bondage and torment.

Forgiveness is to literally be pardoned or spared. *El Nosei*, "the God Who Forgives," is the One who lifts us out of debt. In ancient times livestock was a sign of wealth and prosperity. God's forgiveness is connected to three things in Scripture:

1. He restores our lives.

2. He protects our possessions.

3. He draws us back to His loving-kindness.

When the heavens are shut up and there is no rain because they have sinned against You, when they pray toward this place and confess Your name, and turn from their sin because You afflict them, then hear in heaven, and forgive the sin of Your servants, Your people Israel, that You may teach them the good way in which they should walk; and send rain on Your land which You have given to Your people as an inheritance. When there is famine in the land, pestilence or blight or mildew, locusts or grasshoppers; when their enemy besieges them in the land of their cities; whatever plague or whatever sickness there is...

—I Kings 8:35–37

As a nation, Israel lived under the guidance of God's loving-kindness, even when they served foreign gods. The God Who Forgives always remembers His covenant. *El Nosei* is a covenant-keeping God because He is forgiveness. Psalm 130:3–4 says, "If You, LORD, should mark iniquities, O Lord, who could stand? But there is forgiveness with You, that You may be feared." We are able to stand because God forgives as part of His being. It is not something He does; it is who He is. It is by His Word that He acquits. *Nosei* means, "He bears," or, more literally, "He lifts up" sin. God bears and elevates the sin. This is to say: "My sin is too great to be borne," as seen in Genesis 4:13: "My punishment is greater than I can bear!" It is *El Nosei* who lifted the pronounced punishment from Cain and tailored it. God forgives what we cannot bear.

Love suffers long and is kind; love does not envy; love does not parade itself, is not puffed up; does not behave rudely, does not seek its own, is not provoked, thinks no evil; does not rejoice in iniquity, but rejoices in the truth; bears all things, believes all things, hopes all things, endures all things. Love never fails.

—1 Corinthians 13:4–8

When God's love and forgiveness are combined, people are able to behold Him. These two spiritual ingredients are stirred inside those who accept Jesus as Lord. It is within this lordship, where love is the operating authority, that we are to live. Having a revelation of *El Nosei* is receiving the privilege to know who God is. It is not a right to love God but a command, which gives us the opportunity to interact with the sovereign Creator. People fail to embrace this, resulting in their bearing things that are too great. The yoke of guilt, shame, anger, hurt, and other disruptive feelings causes unnecessary grief. Unforgiveness is like carrying something that weighs more than what we are able to carry. It weakens and tires us over time.

Unforgiveness is spiritually and physically damaging. Forgiveness is the process of ceasing to feel resentment or anger toward another person. It is essential that we learn to forgive and live in a spirit of forgiving at all times. Forgiveness works through our continuous willingness to give up certain claims against a person. A sure way to detect the residue of unforgiveness is when the person is blessed and we do not rejoice for that person. Genuine forgiveness has the ability to celebrate the one forgiven.

Once God forgives, He does not keep score as to how much He has had to endure. "As far as the east is from the west, so far has He removed our transgressions from us" (Ps. 103:12). He says, "For I will forgive their iniquity, and their sin I will remember no more" (Jer. 31:34).

Unforgiveness will destroy families, communities, and even nations. Israel experienced God's judgment when the people went astray. God's healing was always attached to confession of wrong and returning to Him. It becomes important that we recognize the part we play in a situation. We must be willing to totally face up and 'fess up to that part and accept it without blame. We cannot give or receive forgiveness with a fault-finding spirit. This is a spirit that never allows us to recognize our wrongdoings or faults. It is a *finger-pointing demon!*

> Therefore, putting away lying, "Let each one of you speak truth with his neighbor," for we are members of one another. "Be angry, and do not sin": do not let the sun go down on your wrath, nor give place to the devil. Let him who stole steal no longer, but rather let him labor, working with his hands what is good, that

he may have something to give him who has need. Let no corrupt word proceed out of your mouth, but what is good for necessary edification, that it may impart grace to the hearers. And do not grieve the Holy Spirit of God, by whom you were sealed for the day of redemption. Let all bitterness, wrath, anger, clamor, and evil speaking be put away from you, with all malice. And be kind to one another, tenderhearted, forgiving one another, just as God in Christ forgave you.

—Ephesians 4:25–32

THE SPIRIT OF THE VICTIM

There are three barriers that inhibit people from walking in forgiveness:

1. Giving up the hurt
2. Dying to resentment
3. Relinquishing the *right to be right*

Being the *victim* often hides behind *being right*, and it takes a person out of the place of victory. Many find it easier to walk in victimization than to walk in forgiveness, because victimization feeds the flesh. Flesh always desires to promote the fact that *self* is right! The spirit of victimization always roots itself in self-righteousness. Forgiveness waives a person's right to be right.

Self-righteousness can hide behind painful experiences. These experiences cause many to attempt to compensate for what was done to them through subliminal self-pity. Self-pity always leaves the person holding on to the situation in debt. If I am describing your feelings, let's stop and deal with this now.

Yes, it was a terrible thing, and you may have been wronged—but now it's time to get over it! It has been a barrier in your life for too long.

Do not allow it to go to bed with you another night. Wake up in the morning free!

+ Be willing to release all debts from your heart.

+ You do not owe the devil! You do not owe man!

+ You only owe it to yourself to forgive and let go so that you can be *let go*!

+ Let God be right and everything else be considered wrong.

(Before you continue to read, take a moment to talk to God about your experience and your desire to be freed from your *victim* bondage in prayer. Surrender everything to Him—totally.)

God forgave the entire world. While the world was yet sinning, Christ died for us. The God Who Forgives sees us at a completed state, whole and new. To be healed of the past we must be willing to find a new way to think about any person who wronged us. It is a terrible thing to carry the weight of every person, place, or thing that did not do us well. How do we begin to think differently about the worse thing that ever happened in our lives? First, it begins with confessing the right things about the situation. Refuse to rehearse the horror.

When we give burdens to God, it does not just bless us—it blesses everything that concerns us. This is what it means to have the mind of Christ. The mind of Jesus is not to live for self—it is to live for others so they can encounter a loving and forgiving God. One Greek word for *mind* is *phroneo*. It means to have understanding, to feel or to think. The mind of Christ is connected to obedience. When we operate with the same mind that Jesus had, we are obedient to the things of God because we have His sensitive nature. God's nature is responsive to our needs because of His compassion. God's forgiveness moves and removes all those things that hinder us from being who we were created to be in Him.

Forgiveness is an opportunity for healing and growth. It requires a commitment to God's process and season. Forgiveness is not simply a one-time action or an isolated feeling or thought. It involves a change of lifestyle in order to walk with God as Adam did in the beginning. Being not conformed to the world is to know and live the divine will of God in thought, purpose, word, and action. The ultimate goal in being healed from a situation is reconciliation. We must be reconciled (which means to bring balance) within ourselves so that we may be reconciled unto God's divine purpose.

The key to drawing from the anointing of *El Nosei* is sincere confession. When we come clean with God and confess our issues to Him, He forgives us and cleanses us from all unrighteousness (1 John 1:9). When a person does not confess to God the things that are not pleasing to Him, it becomes difficult to walk with the Lord in spirit and in truth. Therefore, true worship becomes impossible.

Mental or physical sickness can be attached to unforgiveness. We must learn to release people, even ourselves, from issues pertaining to unforgiveness so that we may walk in divine health and be mentally whole.

> Is anyone among you sick? Let him call for the elders of the church, and let them pray over him, anointing him with oil in the name of the Lord. And the prayer of faith will save the sick, and the Lord will raise him up. And if he has committed sins, he will be forgiven. Confess your trespasses to one another, and pray for one another, that you may be healed. The effective, fervent prayer of a righteous man avails much.
>
> —James 5:14–16

The effectual prayer of a righteous man avails as a deep and thorough healing of spirit, soul, and body. Prayer assists our mind, will, and emotions to come into agreement with God's desires. The church is called to remain faithful to the plans and purpose of God. The Hebrew word for *Christ* is *Mashiach*. It is the term that literally means "the anointed One." It refers to the ancient practice of anointing kings with oil when they took the throne. Kingship is all about ruling and reigning. Forgiveness is the reign and rule of *El Nosei*, the King (God) Who Forgives. It is *El Nosei* who forgave Israel and who still today seeks to forgive those who call upon His name.

THE NAMES OF GOD IN HEBREW AND ARAMAIC

With the help of my good friend Rabbi Yisrael Avraham, I have listed the names of God in Hebrew and Aramaic. Read these names out in your private time with God. Declare the essence of these names in your life, and healing will come to your heart. Using these names in my prayer time has changed my life, and I pray that they will bless you too![1]

NAMES OF GOD

HEBREW/ARAMAIC NAME OF GOD	ENGLISH MEANING	SCRIPTURE REFERENCE
Shaddai (Sha-di)	Almighty (*Dai*—enough)	Psalm 91:1
Amen (Ah-mayn)	Beginning and the End	Revelation 3:14
Atik Yamim (Ah-teek Yo-meen)	Ancient of Days (Before Time, You Are)	Daniel 7:9
Melekh Panav (Mal-akh Pah-nav)	The Angel of His Presence	Isaiah 63:9

NAMES OF GOD

HEBREW/ARAMAIC NAME OF GOD	ENGLISH MEANING	SCRIPTURE REFERENCE
Lechem Ha Chayim (Lek-khem Khi-yeem)	Bread of Life	John 6:48
Rosh Pinnah (Rosh Pee-nah)	Capstone	Psalm 118:22
Peleh Yoetz (Pe-leh Yo-ayts)	Wonderful Counselor	Isaiah 9:6
Boreh Ketzot Ha-Aretz	Creator of the Ends of the Earth	Isaiah 40:28
Zero 'ot Olam	Everlasting Arms	Deuteronomy 33:27
Melech Olam (Meh-lekh O-lahm)	Eternal King	Jeremiah 10:10
Aviad (Ah-vee-ahd)	Everlasting Father	Isaiah 9:6
El Olam (El O-lahm)	Everlasting God	Genesis 21:33
Avi (Ah-vee)	Father	Psalm 89:26
Avi Ha Ohrot (Ah-vee Ha-m'o-rot)	Father of the Heaven Lights	James 1:17
Elohim Elyon (Eh-lo-heem El-yon)	God Most High	Psalm 57:2
Elohei Kol Nechaman (Eh-lo-hay Khawl Na-kha-mah)	God of All Comfort	2 Corinthians 1:3
Elohei Kol Chen V'Chesed (Eh-lo-hay Ha-he-sed)	God of All Grace	1 Peter 5:10
Elohei Kol Basar (Eh-lo-hay Kawl Bah-sar)	God of All Mankind	Jeremiah 32:27

NAMES OF GOD

HEBREW/ARAMAIC NAME OF GOD	ENGLISH MEANING	SCRIPTURE REFERENCE
Elohei Kol Haretz (Eh-lo-hay Khawl Ha-arets)	God of All the Earth	Isaiah 54:5
Elohim Tzavos (Eh-lo-heem Ts'va-ot)	God of Hosts	Psalm 80:7
Elohei Yisrael (Eh-lo-hay Yis-ra-el)	God of Israel	Matthew 15:31
Elohei Yaakov (Eh-lo-hay Yah-ah-kv)	God of Jacob	Psalm 20:1
Elohei Ahavah V'shalom (Eh-lo-hay Ha-ah-ha-vah V'ha-shalom)	God of Love and Peace	2 Corinthians 13:11
Elohei Avi (Eh-lo-hay Ah-vee)	God of My Father	Genesis 31:5
Elohei Tehillati (Eh-lo-hay T'hee-lah-tee)	God of My Praise	Psalm 109:1
Elohei Tzva'os (Eh-lo-hay Tseed-kee)	God of My Righteousness	Psalm 4:1
Elohei Ha Shalom (Eh-lo-hay Ha-sha-lom)	God of Peace	Romans 16:20
Adonai Adonai Oz Yeshuati (Ado-ni Ado-ni Oz Y'shu-a-tee)	God, the Lord, the Strength of My Salvation	Psalm 140:7
El Nosei (El No-say)	God Who Forgives	Psalm 99:8
Elohei Teshuati (Eh-lo-hay T'shu-a-tee)	God Who Saves Me	Psalm 51:14
Aluf Neurim (Ah-loof N'oo-ri)	Guide of My Youth	Jeremiah 3:4

NAMES OF GOD

HEBREW/ARAMAIC NAME OF GOD	ENGLISH MEANING	SCRIPTURE REFERENCE
Kadosh (Ko-dosh)	Holy	Isaiah 57:15
Kadosh Israel (Ko-dosh Yis-ra-el)	Holy One of Israel	Isaiah 43:3
Makor Mayim Chayim	Fountain of Living Waters	Jeremiah 17:13
Keren Yeshuah (Keh-ren Yeeshe-ee)	Horn of Salvation	Psalm 18:2
Eh-yeh Ah-sher Eh-yeh	I Am Who I Am	Exodus 3:14
Immanuel (Ee-ma-noo-el)	God With Us	Isaiah 7:14
Melehk Yaakov (Meh-lekh Ya-a-cov)	Jacob's King	Isaiah 41:21
El Kanah (El Kah-nah)	Jealous (Jealous God)	Exodus 34:14
Shofet (Sho-fayt)	Judge	Psalm 50:6
Melekh (Meh-lekh)	King	Psalm 10:16
Melekh Olam (Meh-lekh O-lahm)	King Eternal	1 Timothy 1:17
Melekh Ha Kovod (Meh-lekh Ha-ka-vod)	King of Glory	Psalm 24:7–8
Melekh Hamelachim (Meh-lekh Ha M'lah-kheem)	King of Kings	Revelation 19:16
Melekh Ha Goyim (Meh-lekh Ha Goy-yeem)	King of Nations	Jeremiah 10:7

NAMES OF GOD

HEBREW/ARAMAIC NAME OF GOD	ENGLISH MEANING	SCRIPTURE REFERENCE
Seh Elohim (Seh Ha-eh-lo-heem)	Lamb of God	John 1:29
Ohr Yisrael (Or Yis'rah-el)	Light of Israel	Isaiah 10:17
Ohr Ha Olam (Or Ha-olahm)	Light of the World	John 8:12
El Chai (El Khi)	Living God	Psalm 84:2
Adonai (A-do-ni [Yhwh])	Lord	Exodus 6:3
Adonai Elohim (A-do-ni Eh-lo-heem)	Lord God	Genesis 2:4–7
Adonai El Elohim (A-do-ni Ehl Eh-lo-heem)	Lord God of Gods	Joshua 22:22
Adonai Elohei Hashamayim (A-do-ni Eh-lo-hay Hashah-mi-eem)	Lord, the God of Heaven	Genesis 24:7
Adonai Elohei Yisrael (A-do-ni Eh-lo-hay Yis-rah-el)	Lord, the God of Israel	Joshua 24:2
Adonai Elohei Avoteinu (A-do-ni Eh-lo-hay Ah-vo-tay-mu)	Lord, God of Our Fathers	Ezra 7:27
Adonai Nissi (A-do-ni Nee-see)	The Lord Is My Banner	Exodus 17:15
Adonai Echad O'shmo Echad (A-do-ni Eh-khad Oo-sh'mo Ehkhad)	Lord Is One	Zechariah 14:9

NAMES OF GOD

HEBREW/ARAMAIC NAME OF GOD	ENGLISH MEANING	SCRIPTURE REFERENCE
Adonai Shammah (A-do-ni Shah-mah)	The Lord Is There	Ezekiel 48:35
Adonai Elohei (A-do-ni Eh-lo-hi)	Lord My God	Zechariah 14:5
Adonai Tzur (A-do-ni Tsu-ree)	Lord, My Rock	Psalm 144:1
Adonai Tzva'os (A-do-ni Ts'vah-ot)	Lord of Hosts	Isaiah 6:3
Adonai Haadonim (A-do-ni Ha-a-do-neem)	Lord of Lords	Revelation 19:16
Adonai Eloheinu (A-do-ni Eh-lo-hay-nu)	Lord Our God	Psalm 99:5
Adonai Oseinu (A-do-ni O-say-noo)	Lord Our Maker	Psalm 95:6
Adonai Tzidkeinu (A-do-ni Tseed-kay-nu)	Lord Our Redeemer	Jeremiah 26:6
Adonai Rofecha (A-do-ni Rof-eh-kha)	Lord Who Heals You	Exodus 15:26
Adonai Mekeddeshem (A-do-ni M'kah-deesh-khem)	Lord Who Sanctifies You	Exodus 31:3
Adonai Yireh (A-do-ni Yeer-eh)	The Lord Will Provide	Genesis 22:14
Adonai Eloheicha (Ah-do-ni Eh-lo-heh-kha)	Lord Your God	Exodus 20:2

NAMES OF GOD

HEBREW/ARAMAIC NAME OF GOD	ENGLISH MEANING	SCRIPTURE REFERENCE
Abba Avinul (A-baa-vee-nu)	Father Our Father	Romans 8:15
Yotzer Hakol (Yo-tsayr Ha-kol)	Maker of All Things	Jeremiah 10:16
El Gibbor (El Guee-bor)	Mighty God	Isaiah 9:6
Elyon (El-yon)	Most High	Psalm 9:1–2
Haggo'el	Redeemer	Isaiah 41:14
Mashiach Nagid (Ma-shee-ach Na-gid)	Messiah the Prince	Daniel 9:25
Echad (Eh-khahd)	One	Zechariah 14:9
Esh Okhlah (A-sho-ha-lah)	Consuming Fire	Deuteronomy 4:24
Ma'on (Mah-on)	Our Dwelling Place	Psalm 90:1
Adonai Tzuri V'go'al Yhvh	My Rock My Redeemer	Psalm 19:14
Sar Shalom (Sar Sha-lom)	Prince of Peace	Isaiah 9:6
Go'el	Kinsman Redeemer	Isaiah 49:7
Go'el Haddam	Avenger of Blood	1 Samuel 6:20
Ro'eh (Ro-ee)	Shepherd	Psalm 23:1
Or'eh Yisrael (Ro-eh Yis-rah-el)	Shepherd of Israel	Psalm 80:1
Ben David (Ben Dah-veed)	Son of David	Matthew 9:27

NAMES OF GOD

HEBREW/ARAMAIC NAME OF GOD	ENGLISH MEANING	SCRIPTURE REFERENCE
Ruach El (Roo-akh El)	Spirit of God	Job 33:4
Tzur Ma'oz (Tsoor Mah-oz)	Strong Fortress	Psalm 31:2
Migdal Oz (Meeh-dahl Oz)	Strong Tower	Proverbs 18:10
Elohim Emet (Eh-lo-heem Eh-met)	True God	Jeremiah 10:10
Yashar (Ya-shahr)	Upright One	Isaiah 26:7
Peleh (Peh-leh)	Wonderful	Isaiah 9:6
Dvar Elohim (D'vahr Ha'Ehlo-heem)	Word of God	Revelation 19:13
Yah	Yah	Psalm 68:4
El Roi (El Ro-ee)	The God Who Sees Me	Genesis 16:13
Shimcha (Sheem-kha)	Your Name	Psalm 66:4
Hashem	The Name	Leviticus 24:11
Elah Yerushelem (El-li Ye-ru-sha-lem)	The God of Jerusalem	Ezra 7:19

chapter 10

THE WORD

A s I am writing this chapter, I am ministering to so many people with tragedies, calamities, and issues that are hard to deal with. While praying for one young lady, the question came to my mind: "How do people live without Jesus?" How could I have an answer for people without the Lord of lords and King of kings in my life? Professionals go to college for years and do extensive internships. They eventually sit before people with serious problems, ultimately giving them no true hope. In a world where cancer means death, emotional problems mean medication, and failed relationships are eternal, I thank God for the Word of God! People are clueless in times of trouble.

As believers we have the answer on the inside of us. God is a present help in times of trouble. When people are led to Jesus, it is the beginning of a process that breeds new life. This new life does not necessarily delete the trouble, but it takes a load off the mind while God deals with the problem. God always deals through His Word.

One of the greatest-kept secrets in the world is that men were created to worship the Lord! It is impossible to worship Him without having a strong covenant in His Word. I am convinced that many people have unnecessary struggles in their lives because of a deficit of the Word of God. Even believers attempt to serve God without being rooted in His Word. The Word of God is a sure foundation that gives us the ability to stand and endure in the midst of life's greatest challenges.

This chapter is dedicated to scriptural supports for the fact that having covenant in the Word of God is a direct link to emotional and mental stability. If you have been ignorant to this revelation, . it is not too late! Plunge into the Word of God in this chapter, and every area of your life will be touched with the healing power of the Word of God.

Jesus Is the Word

It would be nothing less than a compromise of my faith to start this chapter without declaring that Jesus is the Word. There is no way to God but through His precious blood. He relates to us all we need to know through His Word. Years ago this would seem unnecessary to say because it is so basic in Christianity. Now as we are in the last of the last days, it must be made clear—if you do not come to God through Jesus, there is no salvation! With New Age movements growing by leaps and bounds, antichrist spirits attempt to make believers bite their tongues. *Any* higher power is acceptable, and being radical for Jesus is frowned upon. It is politically incorrect and offensive to make a statement that Jesus is the "only way."

To declare Jesus as Lord is interpreted by some as an attack against other faiths. Well, my position on this matter must be made clear. I believe that every man should have freedom of religion. This is a part of the foundation of our country. God gave man a will so he could have the right to choose. The truth of the matter is that there is a choice—a *right* choice and a *wrong* choice! I believe that it is my responsibility to convince those who will hear of the terrible Day of Judgment coming. This day will not be good for those who choose the wrong faith. I am not addressing denominationalism but lordship! Jesus is Lord!

Heaven and earth will pass away, but not the Word of God (Matt. 24:35). Many people will disagree with what I am saying, and they have a right, but it does not make them right! I am writing this chapter for those who want healing through the power of the Word—Jesus Christ Himself.

If you are reading this book and you are not a Christian, please do not get offended. Hear me out! My words are rooted in the love and compassion I have for you. If you have tried other religions and worshiped other gods, I am soliciting you to try my God, Jesus! If you are a lukewarm believer and have not taken advantage of the benefits of the Word of God, I challenge you to step out into the deep. Everything you need is in the Word of God.

Life is like a prism. How we see things depends on the position we are looking from. It is called a point of view. When I was a street woman and did not know God, my opinions of things were based on that point of view. Now I come to you from the position of the delivered. God has delivered me from a lifestyle that many do not come out of. (Read my book *Delivered to Destiny*.[1]) I have proof that Jesus works—life results! He walked me from a mess to a miracle through His Holy Word. If you are settled with being a Buddhist, Muslim, or Jehovah's Witness, more power to you. But if you know that you are empty, depressed, unresolved, and living life on a spiritual roller coaster, check this chapter out! Experience the power of the Word (Jesus). It brings real-life results.

> In the beginning was the Word, and the Word was with God, and the Word was God. He was in the beginning with God. All things were made through Him, and without Him nothing was made that was made. In Him was life, and the life was the light of men.
>
> —John 1:1–4

When this Bible passage refers to the Word, it speaks of Jesus Himself. He did not just give us only His literal words on paper; He gave Himself. The Word became flesh. He laid down His life so that we could have abundant life. John 10:10 reveals that Jesus came to the world that we could have *abundant* life.

God reveals that Satan came to steal, kill, and destroy. Often people blame God for trouble in their lives. Though God does send trouble, it is not to take away from the quality of life that we have. The devil comes to make us live our lives lower than the standard that Christ died for. People live a lower standard of life because of deception. Deception comes when the Word of God is hidden from us. Second Corinthians 4:3–4 warns us that if the gospel is hidden, it is done so by Satan, who blinds the minds of the people through darkness. As we read earlier:

+ All things were made by Jesus (John 1:3).
+ In Jesus is life (John 1:4).
+ The life in Jesus is the light of men (John 1:4).

Since all of creation was made by Jesus, and we are created beings, there is no real life outside of Him. In Jesus is life, and in that life is the light that we unconsciously seek. All men have darkness inside them when they do not have Jesus. The Word must be applied to every area of our lives. Even as believers, when we neglect the Word of God, our spiritual eye gets filled with evil, and darkness creeps in. Luke 11:34–35 says that when the eye is evil, the whole body is full of darkness. Then it warns us to be careful that the light in us does not become darkness. There are three Greek words for darkness that we must understand.

1. *Skoteinos*—to be opaque and so full of darkness that the truth cannot come in (Luke 11:34)

2. *Skotos*—a shady darkness that causes swindling, lying, and deceiving spirits (Luke 11:35)

3. *Skotia*—to be in an obscure, insipid, shady, shallow, and lukewarm place with the inability to discern (John 1:5)

These are levels of darkness that have one thing in common. They all keep the truth of the Word of God out and allow great deception to come in. People can be in places of deception so long that the truth is not welcomed. John 1:5 teaches that the light can go to dark places, and the darkness still does not comprehend it. This is why men must be brought out of the kingdom of darkness into the marvelous light. (See 1 Peter 2:9.) The *marvelous light* is *thaumastos*, and it means a light to be admired and desired. We must continue to walk in the light of the Word of God. When this is done, people will want what we have. Matthew 24:24 warns us that false christs and false prophets will try to deceive the very elect people of God. The Greek definition for deception in this passage is, "to cause to roam from safety and truth." Jesus is life, and this life brings light that will lead us into eternity.

THE LIGHT OF THE WORD

The Word of God is a lamp to our feet and a light to our path (Ps. 119:105). This means that if we neglect to get into the Word of God, we will begin to walk in the ways of darkness. We receive the Word in many ways:

- ✦ Church attendance
- ✦ Private time in the Word
- ✦ Bible school
- ✦ Directly from God
- ✦ Words of prophecy and exhortation from other believers

It is important that we have a well-balanced intake of the Word of God. Receiving the Word from any one source can inhibit revelation, limit growth, and even open the door to deception. The Word of God must be established out of the mouth of two or three witnesses (Matt. 18:16). This keeps us in the light. Psalm 119:130 tells us that the entrance of the Word of God gives light and understanding to the simple. You do not have to be deep to walk in the light of the Word. We must allow the Word entrance, and its simplicity will make things that are hard to understand easy to grasp. This is why it is sometimes hard for intellectual minds to receive the things of the gospel. First Corinthians 1:23 (AMP) says that to the world the gospel is "unphilosophical nonsense." Some people are so smart and high-minded that they do not allow the entrance of the Word to bring simple understanding. This keeps the Word (Jesus) out of their businesses and professions, and they have to depend on carnal sources. A vicious cycle is put into place:

Intellect → Carnality → Deception (Darkness) → Death

> Now the mind of the flesh [which is sense and reason without the Holy Spirit] is death [death that comprises all the miseries arising from sin, both here and hereafter]. But the mind of the [Holy] Spirit is life and [soul] peace [both now and forever]. [That is] because the mind of the flesh [with its carnal thoughts and purposes] is hostile to God, for it does not submit itself to God's Law; indeed it cannot.
>
> —Romans 8:6–7, AMP

When man attempts to know more than God, it leads down a dark road where there is no light. Where there is no light, there is no life! What we think of as a *mind of our own* can be a hostile weapon against God's Word. Either we are in the Word of God or against the Word of God. This may sound hard-core, but the truth of this revelation will deliver us into the light where we can receive abundant life.

Second Peter 1:19 says that the Word of God is prophetic, and it is sure. We are warned to pay close attention to it as a lamp shining in dark places until the day breaks through the gloom. Verses 20–21 tells us that the Word of God is not limited to personal interpretation or initiated by man. The Word of God was spoken by men, under the inspiration of God, as they were moved by the Holy Spirit.

BASKING IN THE WORD

> I wait for the LORD, my soul waits,
> And in His word I do hope.
>
> —Psalm 130:5

As a pastor and counselor, it would be easy for me to say that Psalm 130:5 is worth a million dollars. How many have a difficult time waiting on the Lord? In all of my life challenges, the main ingredient to every solution was having the ability to *wait*. How do we wait on the Lord? The answer is, by basking in His Word.

The spirit of anxiety runs rampant in the world today. Many hearts are failing from fear. Standing still is so difficult when it seems as though the enemy has us cornered. When trouble comes, the first thing the enemy brings to our minds is to *do something*. However, doing *nothing* is the key.

At the onslaught of some of the worst things that ever happened to me in my life, I heard the Holy Spirit say, "Go lie down and rest!" This torments the devil. When all of hell is breaking loose and we are supposed to be losing our minds, it really makes him mad when we rest before taking any action. I realize that there may be times when we must act on some things right away, but when you can, rest! A tired mind will cause you to take wrong actions. At the inception of an attack, anxiousness immediately sets in to set us up. I have noticed that attacks come to get us out of place. This is when we have to stand still and see the salvation of the Lord. The inability to stand still will incite more confusion, which ignites recurring curses.

CONFRONTATION IS THE BEGINNING OF HEALING.

The enemy loves what I call *runners*. A runner is a person who runs every time a situation arises he or she cannot deal with. The remedy for a runner is basking in the Word of God. When a situation has not been confronted, you will always be faced with a recurring curse. If you live a life of running away from problems, as soon as you stop to rest, the situation will always lift its ugly head again. And no matter how much of a runner you are, eventually you will have to stop and take a breath. This is when reality kicks in.

Confrontation is the beginning of healing. I use the slang phrase, *dealing starts the healing!* Nahum 1:9 tells us that no affliction shall come upon us a second time. When we push things into our subconscious as though they never happened, they follow us, and we are subliminally haunted. A dark cloud rules overhead, and bouts of fear, depression, and all other kinds of emotional stuff arise.

If you are experiencing what I am talking about, rise up, put on the whole armor of God, and confront your situation with the Word of God. Confronting wickedness with the Word cannot be successfully accomplished without the *anointing to wait*. Everything that happens in the natural must happen in the Spirit first. If God does not reveal it, we cannot see things that happen in the Spirit, so we must wait on the manifestation. This is why we walk by faith and not by sight. By faith, we should not be runners. We should stand and confront defiant circumstances with the Word of God. It takes boldness to confront negative issues.

The word *confront* is defined as: to stand face-to-face in hostility and defiance; to stand in front of in total contradiction.

This tells me that to confront something we must be totally in disagreement with it. I believe that you cannot be delivered from what you are in love with. When we are in love with something, we are in total agreement with it. I can specifically relate my point to issues with sin. People have a hard time dealing with sin in their lives because they have not broken covenant with the act. To stop sinning, you have to hate it. You may say that you hate sin, but you do not continually hang out with, sleep with, or eat the things you hate. Personally speaking, I hate spinach! No one has to drill me daily, "Kimberly, stop eating spinach!" The thought of how it tastes makes my face cringe. I do not think about spinach and smile. The things that we are not supposed to do that make our hearts smile must be confronted. What we do not confront we will continually run from.

I spend a lot of time in the life restoration business. I personally minister to people coming out of things like drug addiction, drug dealing, homosexuality, and witchcraft. Though our success rate is high, some do turn back. I have seen this many times, and the signs are always the same. The enemy hates the restoration of lives! If a life is restored to Jesus, Satan will do everything that he can to keep it a secret. This is why we have been instructed that the devil is defeated by the blood of the Lamb and by the word of our testimony.

Jamie is a young man in my ministry who has the most powerful testimony I have ever heard. He was living the fast life on the streets and doing everything that came along with it. The young people with whom he was hanging out were getting shot up in gunfights daily. It was as though they were living in the Wild West. One Sunday, families were passing under the sheaves during our firstfruit offering of the year. Jamie's wife and children were passing under the sheaves as my husband and I prayed.

Jamie had sneaked into the service with no intention of getting his life right with God. He was appeasing his wife, just as he had done before. I called him out and asked him to walk under the sheaves. He shook his head, signifying that he could not. I looked into his eyes and realized that he was under demonic influence. We stopped the ceremony and cast the devil out of him. The devil was not willing to come out, and this was probably one of the most dramatic deliverance sessions my church had seen.

To bottom-line it, Jamie was set free! As we left the church, he was standing at the entrance of the church with a cell phone in his hands, saying, "What do I do about this?" My husband and I had no idea what *this* was, so we took Jamie and his family home with us to counsel with him. I kept the cell phone that night and answered all the calls.

That night Jamie experienced peace for the first time in years. He did not know how to confront the lifestyle that came through the calls on that phone after giving his life to Jesus. He did not get a major breakthrough until he confronted what was calling him on the other side of that line. There was no place for compromise and weaning. He had to deal with it cold turkey.

This life-changing deliverance experience happened for Jamie almost a year ago. The residue of what he came out of still tried to follow him to cause him to be unstable in his ways. The Bible refers to this as a "double-minded man, unstable in all his ways" (James 1:8). The truth is that old things must pass away and all things must become new (2 Cor. 5:17).

Many are walking around carrying a dead man on their backs. The weight of carrying this dead man makes you double minded. Up until recently, Jamie was in denial about his struggle with the old man. He confessed scriptures and pretended that things were good when they were not. Though he tried to fake it around his elders, the fruit of his secret bondage manifested in every area of his life. One day, he even stayed out late and did not go to church. He finally broke down, confessed, and confronted his anxieties. He admitted the thoughts he had of going back to the ways of the past. After submitting himself to godly counsel, God gave him a dream.

Jamie's dream

Jamie saw a little white lamb running through all different kinds of terrains. Demons were shooting at the lamb from the second heaven. The significance of the dream was that the lamb kept running (through different terrains) but was not hit by the arrows being shot from above. Finally, the lamb reached a spot that was as white as he was, and the enemy could not see him from above. A voice yelled from above, "Stay still and do not run!" As the voice shouted to the little lamb, "Stay still," the arrows seemed so close to the lamb that he thought he would be surely hit. Running, in defiance against the voice, the lamb ran out of the white spot and was snatched up into the sky and stood face-to-face with the enemy.

Jamie was awakened.

I do not claim to be an interpreter of dreams, but God clearly gave me the interpretation of this one: The little white lamb represented the righteous. This little lamb was running from circumstances and situations shot at him in life. As long as he was running, the enemy could locate him. When the lamb reached the white place, which represented the will of God, the enemy could not locate him.

Even though we belong to God, we are in trouble if we are out of the will of God. In the will of God, weapons will still form. It will even seem that the enemy's arrows will surely get us. We must realize that the enemy cannot locate us in the will of God, and he is only bluffing and sending taunts. We must stand and confront the taunts of the enemy by staying in place.

We must stay on the wall. When Nehemiah and his men were rebuilding the walls of Jerusalem, Nehemiah was not moved from the wall. He responded to Sanballat, Geshem, and Tobiah's threats by saying, "I am doing a great work, and I am not coming off the wall to see what you want!" (See Nehemiah 6:3.) When we stay in place, the enemy cannot touch us. But we must confront his taunts by continuing the work. If we do not deal with the enemy's taunts *face-to-face* on our turf, we may be snatched up and have to deal on his grounds.

The devil wants to get us out of place because this is the only way he can devour us. Just like the big bad wolf, he will threaten to huff and puff and blow our house down. But when the Word of God is our foundation (floor), our covering (roof), and our walls…who's afraid of the big bad wolf?

Stop running from what God wants to deal with! You can bask in the Word of God and be victorious. Those who wait on God will not be ashamed (Isa. 49:23). I encourage you that if you must run, the name of the Lord is a strong tower; the righteous run into it and are safe (Prov. 18:10).

Unless you are headed for the strong tower of the Lord when you are running, stop, stand still, and *see the salvation of the Lord* (Exod. 14:13).

The Spirit of the Lord GOD is upon Me,
Because the LORD has anointed Me
To preach good tidings to the poor;
He has sent Me to heal the brokenhearted,
To proclaim liberty to the captives,
And the opening of the prison to those who are bound;
To proclaim the acceptable year of the LORD,
And the day of vengeance of our God;
To comfort all who mourn,
To console those who mourn in Zion,
To give them beauty for ashes,
The oil of joy for mourning,
The garment of praise for the spirit of heaviness;
That they may be called trees of righteousness,
The planting of the Lord, that He may be glorified.

—Isaiah 61:1–3

Blessed is the man
Who walks not in the counsel of the ungodly,
Nor stands in the path of sinners,
Nor sits in the seat of the scornful;
But his delight is in the law of the LORD,
And in His law he meditates day and night.
He shall be like a tree
Planted by the rivers of water,
That brings forth its fruit in its season,
Whose leaf also shall not wither;
And whatever he does shall prosper.

—Psalm 1:1–3

PRAYER

Father, we thank You right now for the anointing. We thank You that it destroys the yoke of the enemy. God, we thank You that Your Word is a lamp unto our feet. Guide our paths as we walk through Your Word as you teach us holiness, righteousness, and how to be in right standing with You. Teach us how to be trees of righteousness. I declare that we are planted in the right place by rivers of living water. We are not trying to root ourselves in still waters that run deep.

Jesus, we thank You for those rivers, in the name of Jesus. We thank You that You're stirring up the waters in the Spirit and that we do not have to wait for an angel to come and to stir the waters, in the name of Jesus. Lord, You are stirring waters on the inside of us, and out of our bellies shall flow rivers of living water. Those rivers of living water will bring forth righteousness out of our bellies.

Lord, I thank You that we will not just walk in power, but we will walk in right standing with You. Teach us and show us the deeper things of Your Word. Let Your Word be a flashlight to show us the next step that we should take along the way. David said that his foot almost slipped. God, I thank You that every time he almost fell, there was a light that came from the Word that was on the inside of him. The Word gave him the strength to stand in the midst of adversity, trouble, and tribulation. God, as believers we have many afflictions, but Your Word delivers us from them all. A righteous man will fall down seven times, God, but we get up every time.

I thank You for the anointing to get up. I thank You that I am like Timex—I can take a lickin' and keep right on tickin'. The seed of Your Word is on the inside of my belly, and I am rooted by rivers of living water and grounded in the right place—a place of provision! I am not hanging out in dead and dry places that will cause my roots to wither.

God, because I have strong roots, I have strong fruits. I thank You that You are bringing me into a season where my blessings will no longer be underground because You are displacing everything in my life that is not like You.

I decree and I declare with apostolic authority that You have given me beauty for ashes. You have given me the oil of joy for mourning. You have given me the garment of praise to replace the spirit of heaviness so that I can stand before creation as a tree of righteousness.

God, I thank You right now for everything on the inside of me that lines up with everything on the inside of You. Amen.

chapter 11

DELIVERED FROM
EMOTIONAL DAMAGE

THE SPIRIT OF the Lord comes upon us because God has anointed us for a specific purpose. Many folks do not understand the purpose for the anointing. The anointing is not just to make us look or feel good. The foundational purpose of the anointing is for us to preach the gospel of Jesus Christ under the same power He did. He even went as far to say that we would do greater works than He did (John 14:12).

Spiritually speaking, there are no good preachers! If we were so good in or of ourselves, there would be no purpose for the anointing. We would be ministering by the realm of the flesh. In the story of the young rich ruler, the young man talked to Jesus about being *good*. Jesus responded, "Why do you call Me good? No one is good but One, that is, God" (Mark 10:18). God is the only One who is really good. Even when we have not paid the price to preach or to carry the anointing, God always shows up and shows out. We are not anointed for ourselves, and He doesn't give His anointing to selfish people.

The reason that we have the anointing is not to be puffed up to think more of ourselves than we ought to. We must understand what the anointing is really for. It is for the preaching of the unadulterated truth that is followed by signs and wonders to set the captives free.

> ## THE MINISTRY OF DELIVERANCE, OR THE MINISTRY OF CASTING OUT DEVILS, WALKS HAND IN HAND WITH THE MINISTRY OF INNER HEALING.

I must ask: Why are there so many depressed people in the body of Christ? Why are so many people suffering from anxiety and panic attacks in the body of Christ? I believe that it is because too many do not have a revelation about the stewardship of the anointing.

God anointed us so that people would not have to be depressed. He anointed us so that men and women would not be addicted to mind medication or suffer from mental distress. The sixty-first chapter of Isaiah is not limited to the ministry of casting out devils. It goes further and taps into the realm of inner healing. The ministry of deliverance, or the ministry of casting out devils, walks hand in hand with the ministry of inner healing.

Trauma comes upon a person when that person is oppressed, obsessed, or possessed by any kind of influence from demonic attack. Our bodies were not made to carry devils around in them. We are the temples of the Holy Ghost. Our bodies were made to carry the glory of God on the inside so that the anointing of God would be upon us. Because of this, we can minister to a lost and a dying world to tell them that they need more than Dr. Phil to attain victorious living. God bless people like Dr. Phil and Oprah, but even the help they provide for people means nothing without Jesus Christ. They provide awesome service to the community, but people need results that build strong relationships with God.

Psychiatry and psychology are really not the source for emotional healing. Our answer for every kind of emotional trauma is found in

Isaiah 61, for everything that would come up against our peace and joy is found in the Word of God.

Some of the people who started out in ministry with me failed to grow in their ministries as time went on. They did not allow God to take them to new levels. Ministers who are used by God must have spiritual growth and maturity, which allows an upgrade in their ministry approach. Physicians, lawyers, and many professionals are required to take continuing education courses. They have to keep up with new discoveries and changes. Unfortunately, some ministers do not submit themselves to this principle. The enemy tricks them into believing that they have arrived and need no spiritual or professional growth. Many people overlook the fact that ministers are professionals. We work for the Most High God, and His kingdom reigns over every conglomerate or corporation in the world.

Deliverance (casting out devils) is a foundational part of salvation, but we must build from there. One way we build on deliverance is through inner healing. We must do more than call demons out of people with broken hearts and contrite spirits. They need inner healing.

New revelation is even more important to ministers than to regular professionals. When dealing in the spirit we deal with eras of devils. Demons are not limited to operating regionally. They are strategically assigned according to the eras of their times. There was a time when Dagon was a prince of the devils. Before Dagon, Baal held the position of his era. Then, in the time of Jesus, Beelzebub was the prince of the devils. Because chief spirits rule by era, we must be able to flow according to the time we walk in. Dealing with the princes of Baal's time requires a different approach than dealing with the princes of Dagon's time. There has to be a spiritual upgrade.

God brings increase as we are faithful over little. He'll make us ruler over much, and He's not going to give us more until we are faithful over what He has already given.

The anointing comes upon us to set the captives free. I know this to be a fact because Jesus stood in the temple and read it. (See Luke 4:16–19.) Many didn't understand the anointing in which He walked. They didn't understand a Messiah who didn't show off with a hundred armor bearers carrying Him around on a shoulder-mounted throne. He wasn't carried in on a golden carriage. He showed up on a donkey and confused everybody.

Jesus wanted the reason that He came to be understood by everyone. He was a "sent one"! As God sends His anointed out, people must understand that where they came from is not important. The urgency is that we know why we came—*to set the captive free!* God is dealing with the purposes and motives we have for the ministry we do.

Traumatic Experiences

Trauma can be defined several ways:

+ A deeply disturbing experience that produces psychological injury or pain

+ A psychological wound that creates long-lasting damage

+ A shock or attack against the mind from a negative experience, which causes distress and disruption of life

All of these definitions summarize one thing: trauma affects a person to the point of making it impossible to have a victorious life; it inflicts a bite from the "serpents" of life, and the poison injected is worse than the actual bite.

Many times we deal with the entry points of the arrows of the enemy when we need to deal with the poison that the arrows have released. We cannot just put salve on the wounds and fail to deal with the slow-killing effects of the poison from the tainted arrow. The aftereffects of deliverance can leave trauma. There is a residue of the bondage that must be dealt with. Most of the time, this residue comes with a spirit of bondage.

The Bible speaks of the spirit of heaviness in Isaiah 61:3. This word *heaviness* is *keheh* in the Hebrew. It means "spirit of darkness." Many people live their life under a dark cloud. They are depressed, despondent, and have no joy. Depression always accompanies heaviness. The two always walk hand in hand. An underlying root spirit of depression is fear. Fear is the opposite of faith. Faith cannot abide where there is no light.

Second Timothy 1:7 reminds us that God has not given us a spirit of fear but of power, love, and a sound mind. Fear is related to an unstable mind and in direct opposition against a sound mind. The Bible does not say that fear is a diagnosis of a medical disorder; it is a spirit!

The reason society is not gaining ground on the issues of emotional and mental illness is because they have not recognized them for what they are. Fear is a spirit! Depression is a spirit! Anxiety is a spirit! We are dealing with spirits, and whenever you have a devil problem, you need a Jesus answer! This is not real deep. We cannot solve a devil problem with a carnal answer because the carnal things will always come up against the truth.

> **FEAR IS RELATED TO AN UNSTABLE MIND AND IN DIRECT OPPOSITION AGAINST A SOUND MIND.**

Another spirit that I frequently encounter in healing sessions is the spirit of anxiety. Fear gives birth to anxiety. Being anxious causes physical manifestations that lead to insanity. The physical attacks of anxiousness are called panic attacks. Some of the manifestations of panic attacks are:

+ Fast heart rate
+ Shortness of breath
+ Obsession
+ Fear of dying
+ Equilibrium imbalance
+ Insomnia

These physical attacks often lead to insanity because they make the person feel as if he or she is losing his or her mind. Panic attacks are demonic. The strongman of panic attacks is a demon called *Pan*. Pan is the god of fear. He has a human torso and legs like a goat, and he carries a harp or lyre in his hand. I have actually met this demon in a dream. After I saw the spirit, I began to do research on it. While looking through the dictionary, I exclaimed, "This is the demon I saw in the dream."

Pan is the strongman of the center of hell, pandemonium. He is the god of chaos, confusion, and fear. Pan is a mythological creature. But what is mythological? Scientific minds refer to those things they cannot prove by science as a *myth*. By revelation, I know that Pan is the strongman of panic attacks, anxiety, and fear. A person who never comes out of a panic attack will live a tormented life of mental anguish and may eventually become insane. Any time the heart and the mind are panicked, the body cannot operate normally, and there will be no abundant life.

Every person does not handle trauma in the same way. Instead of anxiety, some people may suffer from a spirit of heaviness. The spirit of heaviness is the opposite of the spirit of fear. The end of heaviness is death. Just as Pan is the strongman of fear, the Grim Reaper is the strongman of death. I've also met this demon. He wears a dark hooded garment and carries a sickle in his hand. This is the literal spirit of death.

When I think of the Grim Reaper, I remember the experience my aunt Lillie Mae had with him. She went to be with the Lord years ago. This experience happened when I was in Germany and had just gotten saved. Before my aunt was saved, she was the kind of woman who drank liquor, smoked cigarettes, and read the Bible—all at the same time. She was the only one who took us to church every now and then when I was growing up. It was a Baptist church, and the deacons would stand in the front entrance smoking cigarettes. I cannot remember them ever teaching on holiness. They definitely did not believe in casting out devils.

My aunt always kept the pastor informed of my accomplishments throughout my athletic career. He was always nice to me, that is, until I became a preacher. This turned his kind smile and nice words to a frown with strong criticism. After getting saved, I tried to tell my aunt, who was a faithful (cussing and hell-raising) church member, how I had received the baptism of the Holy Ghost. Of course, she did not want to hear this. She had been in church, as she knew it, all her life. Who was I to tell her about God? But because I loved her so much, I still told her about the Holy Ghost and the devil no matter how mad it made her.

So you can imagine how it caught me off guard when I received news in Germany that she had experienced a stroke and was dying. I told the Lord, "God, she is not saved!" I cried out to Him because I knew that she did not know Him and was religiously on her way to hell. God stayed the hand of death, but my aunt could not speak normally after the stroke. Her speech was drastically impaired. She kept saying, "Get

Kimberly," to family members out of the side of her mouth. She begged for me to come to the hospital, and I flew to Florida from Germany. (I was in the military at the time.)

When I reached the hospital, she was shaking and her eyes were as big as saucers. She kept repeating to me, "Sa-tan...Sa-tan...Sa-tan!" This was coming from the woman who knew nothing about the devil and had become mad at me whenever I mentioned things about the devil in the past. Now she did not merely call him *the devil*, she called him by name, Satan! (When she pronounced his name it sounded like Sa-ton.)

This really got my undivided attention. My aunt had an old lady who was an alcoholic as her roommate. There was never a time when she was not drunk. With stammering words, my aunt began to tell me, "The clock stopped...Sa-ton...the clock stopped...Sa-ton!" She pointed to her roommate to tell me what had taken place the night of the stroke. She kept saying, "She see too...she see too!"

When I talked to her roommate about it, she explained, "Something happened in our house that night. Your aunt was pouring coffee. And all of the sudden, she just started pouring the coffee on the table and looking crazy. She stumbled to her room. I tried to follow her, but angels stood at the door. There were two big men in white standing at the door. When I was trying to go into the room where she was, something flew out of the room. It was the death angel."

It amazed me that these two old ladies, who had known nothing about the spirit realm or spiritual warfare before this incident, were telling me now about a death spirit. I'll never forget their words. Something happened in my aunt's room that night, and I believe that God gave me a revelation of what it was.

As I was interceding for my aunt's soul, God sent angels to cast that death spirit out. She had a stroke in the natural, physical realm, but in reality she was caught between two spirit realms. This is why the clock stopped; her time was up! The devil (Sa-ton) tried to take my aunt to hell. God allowed the alcoholic lady to see it so that I would know that it really happened. The spirit realm is more real than the natural. We must die to our flesh to know this. We cannot be natural (minded) men.

I believe God has revealed to me that strokes have supernatural manifestations. Through this experience, God revealed to me the spiritual significance of a stroke. When our natural bodies are caught between the physical and spiritual realms, our bodies respond with physical defects such as paralysis, impairment, or slurring of speech. It is a traumatic experience to get stuck between two realms. Although many people may dispute this revelation I received, I believe it is because they have not grown in their spiritual experience to the point of having eyes to see and ears to hear the things of the spirit.

I have a friend who was involved in homosexuality for years before he also had a stroke. He was working at a hospital when the stroke occurred and was admitted immediately. When they put him in a bed, he looked up at a giant windowpane in the hospital on the sixth floor and saw the devil floating in the air outside the window. Just before this happened, my friend had been calling on Jesus. The devil told him to shut up because Jesus would not hear him. The devil said, "I've got you now; you are mine!"

My friend ignored the devil's taunts and continued to call on Jesus in repentance, in spite of the sinful lifestyle he had been living. God heard his prayer that night and healed his body supernaturally. As he told the story, I could tell that he too had met the devil while having a stroke.

Many of the things that we try to figure out psychologically or medically are spiritual problems—and often demonic in nature. The Holy Spirit is the only One who can deliver us from a demonic attack. The devil attacks our mind, will, intellect, emotions, and even our natural body functions. If he can influence the mind, the body can begin to function improperly. Before our mouths can speak or our legs walk, there must be neurological transmissions from the brain to other parts of our bodies. The brain controls every other part of our body. Emotional and mental distress can cause physical impairment of the body. This is called a *psychosomatic disorder*. It is an emotional factor that influences the body to cause physical symptoms or disorders.

> **MANY OF THE THINGS THAT WE TRY TO FIGURE OUT PSYCHOLOGICALLY OR MEDICALLY ARE SPIRITUAL PROBLEMS— AND OFTEN DEMONIC IN NATURE.**

Sound mental health is important for every area of our lives. Two Greek words are important in relation to this fact:

1. *Ophthalmos haplous*—sound eye (Luke 11:34)
2. *Ophthalmos poneros*—diseased or evil eye (Luke 11:34)

Our minds are renewed by what we allow to enter our ear and eye gates. We often speak of having ears to hear, but we must also have eyes to see. The two states of a person's vision listed above are the difference between life and death. It is the will of God that we have sound, good eyes. This is the only means by which we may experience renewal of the mind.

> The lamp of the body is the eye. Therefore, when your eye is good, your whole body also is full of light. But when your eye is bad, your body also is full of darkness.
>
> —Luke 11:34

It is made clear that our eyes allow the light in. Diseased or evil eyes deny the body light. When there is no light, darkness will rule. As I mentioned earlier, darkness and depression walk together as close friends.

The rich young ruler asked Jesus about what was *good* (Matt. 19:16–17). The word *good* in reference to having a good eye is *agathos*, and it means:

1. To be agreeable with the things of God
2. To have a good nature
3. To walk upright
4. To be honorable
5. To be joyful

A good eye is mandatory to have a sound mind. Without a sound mind, there is no possible way to obtain abundant life. The reason most people are suffering from attacks against their minds is because they will not allow God to renew them. Their brain is sending the wrong transmissions to their bodies. The spirit and the flesh are battling over the mind. That which controls the mind controls the body.

For years saints have argued over the issue of whether a Christian can have a demon or not. This is frivolous! What difference does it matter if people have demons or not if the demon has their minds? The body will always follow the mind. This is why young boys do not have to get into the panties of a young girl. They just have to get into her mind. You see, if they can get into her mind, entrance into the panties is inevitable.

The plan of the enemy is to get into our minds. If he can get into our minds, he can get anything else he wants from us. If the devil can get into your mind, he can get your money. If he can get into your mind, he can destroy the marriage to which you said you would always be faithful. If he can get into your mind, he can take the healing that God promised you. I don't care how many Scriptures we quote; we need the Word of God rightfully appropriated in areas of our lives so that we can experience the benefits of a renewed mind.

Unrenewed minds are subject to the spirit of fear. Romans 8:15 talks about how fear is a spirit of bondage. Some people take being afraid lightly. There are different types of fear in the Bible, but God talks about the spirit of fear in 2 Timothy 1:7. The Greek word for *fear* is *deilia*, which means "timidity." God has not given us a timid spirit. You may think of fear as just being scared of the boogeyman. No, spiritual fear makes you afraid to step out, afraid to deal with or to confront things according to the will of God. It will make you lean toward taking the nice or easy way out of things.

Many people want the quiet way out of problems. I have learned that when God really deals with our hearts about an issue, He generally busts us out! His correction is loud! Sometimes He puts us front and center so we can deal with things we are timid or shy about. The kingdom of God suffers violence, and God demands that we take what is ours by force (Matt. 11:12). Mental and emotional health must be taken by force. We must stand in *holy boldness*. The spirit of timidity is the opposite of boldness. We are dealing with a bold devil, and if we tiptoe through the tulips with the devil, we will be beaten down in life.

When Joshua was sent in to possess the land of a foreign nation, God wanted him to be bold, strong, and of great courage. We cannot be shy about the things of God or about the power of God. We must be bold about the truth, and the truth is that timidity is a sin. Timidity is from the devil, and I would not receive it because it is not from God. I don't want anything that God has not given me.

The spirit of timidity walks down the aisles of churches every Sunday. This spirit also operates from the pulpits. The spirit of timidity will not deal with darkness. It is a nice/nasty demon of deception that hides under the cloak of false submission to God. If we do not deal with darkness, somebody is going to stay bound up. I do not want that blood on my hands!

THE SOLUTION TO THE PROBLEM

Many people have been in the church for a long time without proper training. The fivefold ministry is for the equipping of the saints. People should not have to attend Bible schools or seminaries for basic believer training. We need to deal with *stuff* in our congregations. Many pastors are so timid that they are afraid to deal with issues like lesbianism and homosexuality. We have pretended that the church is a beautiful building with perfect people for so long that God has been using the world to bust us out.

Things that should have been dealt with inside the walls of the church are being dealt with on CNN and FOX News. This is not the time to be ashamed of dealing with touchy issues. If we back up in timidity, we will really be shamed in the end. The Spirit of God comes upon us to deal with nasty dirty issues like molestation, masturbation, and incest.

We should not hesitate to deal with transsexuals, transvestites, homosexuals, and pedophiles. All of these people are suffering from demonic attacks that have affected them mentally, emotionally, and even physically. Some consider these kinds of people to be the scum of the earth. Actually, they are the very people Jesus came to die for and the people for whom He was anointed. He came for the transvestites...He came for the lesbians...and He came for the mass murderers. He came to set them free!

It doesn't matter how bad your situation is as you are reading this book. The anointing is more powerful than your dirty and low situation. The anointing destroys the powers of darkness. Do not be timid about your healing. Allow Jesus to transform your mess into a miracle!

Pray with me as I pray this prayer over you:

> I break the powers of darkness off your mind, right now, in Jesus's name! I command the light to be strong in your eyes so that your body can be whole. Let the light come! I command the darkness of depression and the confusion of anxiety to go! Every psychosomatic disorder that has affected your life must bow to the blood of Jesus. Every psychic attack, physical attack, spiritual attack, social attack, emotional attack, financial attack, or material attack is bound and blocked forever in Jesus's name. The residue from trauma is dried to the roots, and the wounds are healed, down to your literal spirit man. The anointing destroys every yoke in your life…in Jesus's name. Amen.

Do not forget that you can never be bold about what you are not sure of. In this case you will operate in bold ignorance.

Another reason that people find themselves in mental and emotional messes is because of a lack of spiritual discipline. I met the *spirit of discipline* in the United States Army. In Germany, I learned how to move in the spirit. I thanked God for a solid foundation. The elder women that God put in my life did not really cast out demons as I did, but they were walking in *something* in God. I will never forget looking at them and admiring the authority in which they walked. They would tell me, "Shut up and sit down. That's not the Lord, baby. Sit your behind down!"

I never thought to be offended. I believe that this was because I wanted what they had. I didn't have time to be distracted by offense. I knew the love that they had for me, and I understood that they didn't mean me any harm. When they were moving in the Spirit, if I was standing in the wrong place, they would say, "Get your behind over here. You have no business over there. Move out of the way."

When these women prayed, I saw signs, wonders, and miracles. In the midst of Operation Desert Storm, in the midst of real war, we weren't playing—we were praying! This was no play-play stuff at the time. We were in a real war situation. The Germans had signs all around us, "Americans, go home." We could not play with prayer. We had to be in place, and timidity was not an option. This was one of the hardest times of my life.

> OH, HOW I LONG FOR THE DAY WHEN THE SAINTS WILL TAP INTO THE VEIN OF GOD TO UNDERSTAND THAT THE SICK AND THE OPPRESSED NEED TO BE SET FREE!

During this time, weekly Bible study meant something! When I went to my cell group with everything weighing down heavily on my back, I never left the same. No matter what was going on in my life, someone always had a prophetic word, a song, or a scripture that would encourage my soul. They would say, "Sister, this is what I see. This is what's going on." God didn't use just one person; He used everybody. I think that was an example of what being in the body of Christ is all about. People were equipped! To be equipped, we must have spiritual discipline.

In Germany, every service was flowing with interpretation of tongues, words of knowledge, and words of wisdom. A standard was set, and everybody walked in it.

Today, churches are full of superstar ministers. Everybody wants to be Ms. Deliverance and Mr. Prophet. This is why a whole lot of bumping and grinding is going on in the church. The Spirit of God cannot really flow because everybody is trying to do his or her own thing. Oh, how I long for the day when the saints will tap into the vein of God to understand that the sick and the oppressed need to be set free! People are either being regenerated in the Spirit, or they are degenerating because of the flesh.

Degeneration

When the flesh takes hits, the spirit of a man gets worse. This is how a wounded spirit is attained. The state of the man gets worse. The demon keeps coming in and out of the flesh. Every time that demon comes back again, the spirit gets weaker, and weak spirits lead to wounded spirits.

A lot of people live by and are satisfied with the *diagnosis* (fruits) of a problem. They do not care to deal with the *epignosis* (roots or full understanding of the problem). The diagnosis is based on symptoms and manifestations. Diagnosis (of a natural source) has taken the place of discernment (of a spiritual source). We do need both, but the things of the spirit must come first.

In the military, every soldier knew how to troubleshoot a problem. We could troubleshoot anything from a car to a person. We had charts and schematics to guide us from the problem to the answer. The chart would say, "If a person has a runny nose, red eyes, and itchy ears," across from the symptom would be the answer: "ear infection."

The Holy Spirit is the ultimate troubleshooter. God made us so wonderfully and so beautifully individual—we do not have the same fingerprints or footprints. The makeup of a person is so unique, yet the Holy Spirit can put His finger on our issues without any mistakes. Some people may share the same symptoms, but the root problems are different. This is what society is doing wrong. People are troubleshooting lives based on the schematics of the world. God made man, and He knows how to fix every part of every person when we break down.

When Jesus deals with a problem, He puts the ax to the root (Matt. 3:10). He went to the *epignosis*! He didn't just check out the fruit. When Jesus gets through solving a problem, it's gone forever. The world attempts to fix our life-or-death issues by just putting rubbing alcohol and Band-Aids on the problem. The world has taught us to medicate people with demonic problems to pacify their flesh. One of the things that irk me most is seeing a person who is tormented by demons being stroked (in a service) and told that everything is going to be all right.

> **THE HOLY SPIRIT IS THE ULTIMATE TROUBLESHOOTER.**

Can you imagine how God feels? This may be the *churchy thing* to do, but it does not set the captives free. People don't need to hear, "It's going to be all right." They need the devil pulled out of them. They need supernatural intervention from God. Jesus didn't stroke or counsel devils. Jesus cast out devils, and He was bold about it.

At one point in His ministry, Jesus received a message that Herod was going to kill Him. I love the way Jesus responded:

> And He said to them, "Go, tell that fox, 'Behold, I cast out demons and perform cures today and tomorrow, and the third day I shall be perfected.'"
> —Luke 13:32

Jesus said, "What? They are going to kill me? I came to die—make My day! You don't cast me out; I cast out devils!"

What preacher would say, "I don't cast out devils"? One who does not really understand what it means to be like Jesus. We cannot walk around with a spiritual question mark over our heads asking, "What would Jesus do?" We must do what Jesus did! He set the captives free!

The spirit of religion has been manifesting in church folk for a long time. It manifested in John the Baptist when he was in prison. At first he was rebuking and baptizing everybody, but as soon as trouble came, he questioned the fact that Jesus was the Messiah. Like he baptized the wrong one? Like God was confused when He said Jesus was His Son and He was pleased with Him? John asked Jesus, "Are you the Coming One, or do we look for another?" (Luke 7:19).

Jesus said, "What changed? Go tell him that the blind eyes are being opened up, the sick are being healed, and the dead are raised. I am the One who came to set the captives free!" (See Luke 17:22–23.)

When Jesus came into contact with people with issues, they did not stay the same. Why do we have churches today where most people stay the same? They might as well be social clubs. The church is supposed to be the mental floor of the hospital. The pews should be an emergency room. The world does not do a good job at the work the church was birthed to do.

The backsliding spirit is rampant in the church. When people keep going back and forth in God, they get wounded. Their spirit gets wounded. A wounded spirit causes the heart to get bitter. Bitter hearts live in the past, and they can never go forward. You can discern a bitter heart by listening to a person's conversation. When that person is still talking about things that people did to him or her twenty years ago, he has the *spirit of the victim*. God says we are more than conquerors.

He didn't say we were victims. People with victimized mind-sets like it when others feel sorry for them. God did not call us to walk in sorrow. Any sorrow or pity, outside of godly sorrow, is a spirit. I call it *sympathetic magic*.

INFIRMITY OF THE SPIRIT

Infirmity can manifest in other ways than through the flesh. If you have a wounded spirit, then infirmity can get in your spirit. When a person has a wounded spirit, the spirit man is literally slumped over. I have seen this in the spirit, and the person looks as though he or she is spiritless! They cannot move forward. A spiritless person is a person with no hope. Without hope we can never have faith. What faith am I going to have if I have nothing to look forward to? Hope is that which looks forward to tomorrow. If you have no hope in tomorrow, you can't have faith in today.

> The spirit of a man will sustain his infirmity; but a wounded spirit who can bear?
> —Proverbs 18:14, KJV

It's important to have a strong spirit. Your life can be saved with a strong spirit. It destroys infirmity! Even cancer cannot stay in a person with a strong spirit. Many people die early because they lose the desire to live. Their spirit man is so weak that they have no zeal left for life.

I witnessed this a year ago with my natural father. He lost his bar in the downtown area of my city. In my book *Delivered to Destiny* I called this place "Uptown." My brother was arrested for possessing cocaine on the property, and my father lost his liquor license. He had been the first black man in our city to obtain this kind of license. After this incident, my father stopped paying taxes on the bar property. It was worth over a million dollars. The location was in the center of downtown Jacksonville, Florida. The city took the property. My father lived the rest of his life lying on a sofa bed in his living room in the projects in my city. He rarely laughed, and he never drove past the property again. We could not even discuss it with him. I did lead him to the Lord, but he eventually died on that sofa of a broken heart. Sickness after sickness attacked his body, but he willed to die. His spirit could not sustain his infirmity.

Before cancer can ever get in your spirit, it has to get into your mind. Remember that everything goes through the mind. Your mind will inject that wound to your spirit. This is why folks who are messed up in their minds ultimately get despondent and down in their spirits. A person who is down in his or her spirit will eventually be susceptible to physical infirmity.

> My days are past,
> My purposes are broken off,
> Even the thoughts of my heart.
> They change the night into day;
> "The light *is* near," they say, in the face of darkness.
>
> —Job 17:11

What happens when your night changes into day? That means you are not getting any sleep. Who can sleep in bright light? I have two birds in my home, and in order for them to rest, we have to put a dark cover over the cage. If we do not cover the cage, the birds will think it is day and chirp all night. As human beings, we need the night. There is a purpose for the day, and there is a purpose for the night. The purpose for the night is to rest.

Job said, "Rest has left me. The dark that I need has left me. There's a bright light in my head that won't let me sleep, and my night has become day." When people cannot sleep, break the *bird curse* off of them. When light comes, birds begin to chirp. At night they are quiet and rest. The bird curse is when the discernment of the human body is out of order and night becomes day. Break the power of the lights in their heads that never go off, and cover their nights with the blood of Jesus, just as I cover my birds. God will give them sweet sleep and divine rest. It is a curse for the beloved of God to have no sleep. Command the racetrack and the hustle of the day to cease in their minds so that they can have mental rest.

> If I make my bed in the darkness...
> Where then is my hope?
> —Job 17:13, 15

Some people may need to repent of things they have done to cause darkness to come upon them. In Job's case, he said that he made his bed in a place of darkness. There is no hope when we have unrepented sin in our lives. The word *hope* means "expectancy." Job was actually saying, "Where is my expectancy?"

This word *hope* is *tiqvah*. It means, "I expect nothing." A lot of people are walking around expecting nothing because of the spirit of condemnation. Repentance is the key. There is no condemnation for those who are in Christ Jesus and have sense enough to repent.

> Now faith is the substance of things hoped for...
> —Hebrews 11:1

We cannot have the substance of faith if we have no hope. The word *substance* is so important when it comes to faith in God. Because we walk by faith and not by sight, substance helps us with what we cannot see. Substance is defined as "the tangible manifestation of faith

161

that causes the actual matter of a thing to oppose the mere shadow of it." Circumstances and situations hide the tangible manifestations of God's promises from our minds and breed doubt. I do not literally have to possess what I am believing God for, but the reality and the manifestation of it are rooted in my heart by the substance of my faith. Because of this, I have hope. I have heard many preachers say, "I am not hoping for anything; I believe God!" I do not think that this is real biblical faith. If we fail to hope, we cannot believe. Hope cannot be separated from faith.

A Broken Heart and a Contrite Spirit

The Lord is near to those who have a broken heart,
And saves such as have a contrite spirit.

Many are the afflictions of the righteous,
But the Lord delivers him out of them all.
He guards all his bones;
Not one of them is broken.
Evil shall slay the wicked,
And those who hate the righteous shall be condemned.
The Lord redeems the soul of His servants,
And none of those who trust in Him shall be condemned.
—Psalm 34:18–22

Is there a light on your feet? If you don't know your way, you can let the flashlight of the Word walk you through darkness. *Yea, though I walk through the shadow of death, I will fear no evil.* We cannot fear evil when God is walking with us. He is close to those with a broken heart and a contrite spirit.

I was looking up the term "broken heart." The word *heart* is *leb* in Hebrew. It means "feelings, mind, will, and intellect." It refers to those who are broken in feelings. The word *broken* literally means "to crush your view." God is especially close to those who can't see straight and to those who have been hurt so badly that their view has been crushed. These are the kinds of people God is close to.

> **WE CAN BE HELD BACK, DESPONDENT, DEPRESSED, AND HELD DOWN IN THE SPIRIT BECAUSE OF A WOUNDED SPIRIT.**

He's close to those with a contrite spirit. To have a broken heart is to have your feelings crushed to the point that you can't see straight. The word *spirit* is *ruwach*, which means, "the wind of God." Things come in life that literally knock the wind of God out of us. The devil knows that if we can just breathe, we will be all right. Oppression takes a person's ability to breathe. I have prayed for many people who seem to have a tight tube around their chest. This is a python spirit that tightens whenever the person tries to get a release. Just like the natural creature, this spirit allows air to flow in, but it will not allow a person to exhale. Many people are really living their lives waiting to exhale. The word of the Lord is that they need more than relief—they need a release!

The hardest thing for me to get people to see is that demons cannot get into our spirit. Demons operate through the flesh realm, and witchcraft is a work of the flesh. Read the chapter on witchcraft in my book *Give It Back!*[1] We can be held back, despondent, depressed, and held down in the spirit because of a wounded spirit. It's not about a demon being in the spirit—it is possible that people with wounded spirits have demons in their flesh. Either the demon has been there and now is gone, or the demon is residing there now and needs to be dealt with.

We need to deal with the demonic arrows that have wounded people in their minds, and the wounds have gotten down in their spirits. A person with a crushed and collapsed spirit is unstable in all of his or her ways. Listen to the conversation of the person. Such a person will say one thing one moment, and in the next minute say something totally opposite. This is a manifestation of a person with a contrite spirit. A godly counselor does more than give good advice. He or she has an ear in the spirit to hear what is going on with a person while that person is expressing himself or herself.

A MERRY HEART

"A merry heart makes a cheerful countenance" (Prov. 15:13). This means that people who go around mean, ugly, nasty, and sad do so because something in their hearts is not merry. A merry heart will make a joyful face. Understanding this will help us not to be so easily offended when someone looks at us in a negative way or even forgets to speak. A lot of folk are lashing out at others because they are simply miserable, and they need ministry. Do not work with the devil against these individuals. They are sick at heart! You need to stand in the gap and pray for them. They may be about to lose their minds, and they could be suicidal. Be the more spiritual person.

Recently I saw a very famous comedian in an airport. The Lord began to speak to me about him. I could tell that he could go off on a person, but God gave me a word for him. I was not impressed with who he was. I do not even like his show. The Lord quickened me to call a friend of mine who is an actress in Hollywood. The Lord said that she would know him. God told me to call her and give the phone to him. Just as I thought he would be, he was very short with me, but I obeyed the Lord. My friend told him who I was, and the ice was somewhat broken.

It was just like the Lord to arrange that we were even seated close to each other in the first-class cabin of my flight that day. I could not get his attention long enough to prophesy to him, so I wrote the prophecy on paper. I touched him to give the prophecy to him as he attempted to pretend that he did not feel me touching him. I gave him the paper and shook the dust off of my feet. It took everything in me not to get mad at him.

After a four-hour plane ride, he turned around and started thanking me for the prophetic word. He said that it was on time. I said a lot to him, but the main thing I told him was that he was depressed. He was a popular comedian. One of his themes was based on laughter bringing healing, yet he was depressed himself. I ministered to him, and he admitted that he was depressed. I told him he could only make people laugh; he could not give them true joy. He could not give what he did not have. No one can release real joy to people without Jesus Christ in his or her life. This is why most comedians have to curse and use profanity to be funny. When they do not have God's help, they have to rely on the devil's help.

Proverbs 17:22 also talks about a merry heart: "A merry heart does good, like medicine." That means that a merry heart stimulates the body in the right way. A merry heart stimulates the body and heals like medicine. If a merry heart can heal us, then a sad heart can bring sickness and disease.

When I was first saved, I used to see a lot of visions. One particular vision that I had was about people getting filled with the Holy Ghost. I saw some little men who looked like gingerbread men, with their hands and arms and legs held out in the air as if they were praising God. Some of them were filled to the waist with blue water. In some of them the blue water filled them to the chest. Others were filled with blue water all the way to the top of their heads. And depending on the level of the blue water that was in them, that's how far their arms went up as they praised God. The gingerbread men who were filled with the blue water to the tops of their heads held their hands up the highest. I know today that blue water represented the Holy Spirit, who is the only one who can bring real joy. Blue is a color for authority. Our level of praise affects our level of joy, which affects our level of authority.

With this vision, God was showing me the reason why a lot of people can't praise God. Rivers of living water are not flowing out of their bellies. Rivers of joy cannot flow out of us until we are filled with the Holy Spirit with the evidence of speaking in other tongues. I am saying that people cannot have the joy of the Lord without the infilling of the Holy Ghost... YES! God commanded us to "be filled with the Spirit" (Eph. 5:18). That means overflowing. The little men who were filled to the top were zealous about the things of the Lord. You may have received the Holy Ghost, but did you get filled? He didn't just say receive the Holy Ghost and stop there. He said, "Be filled with the Spirit."

God also showed me how some people who may have been filled can begin to leak due to a weak spirit. Although they receive from God, the enemy comes immediately to cause it to leak out. This is why we need strong spirits to contain the glory of God on the inside of us.

When people go around mean, ugly, never happy, and can't joke, they are telling on themselves. What they are really saying is, "I am miserable, and I do not have enough of God in my life to have joy." It's not that people in this situation hate everybody else—they just don't like themselves. They are saying, "I hate me." To be a hater, you have to first hate yourself. When you love yourself, you can love other people. The reason why we have so many haters is because so many people hate themselves. Hating yourself is a form of suicide.

Idolatry and a lot of other sins are rooted in *the hatred of self*. Such people are discontented and unsatisfied with life. Do you fall in this category? You believe your legs are not big, or small, enough. Your hair is not long, or short, enough. Your teeth are a little too long or too yellow. The devil will pick something all day long to make us hate ourselves. Fat people want to be skinny. Skinny people want to be fat. Light-skinned people want to be dark skinned, and dark-skinned people want to be light. Everybody is striving to be someone else because they subliminally hate themselves. To be filled with the Spirit of God means to be content with who you are.

chapter 12

ADDRESSING THE ISSUE OF
SEXUAL PERVERSION

ANY PEOPLE ARE emotionally distraught because they have experienced sexual encounters outside of the plan of God for their lives. As a result, they cannot pull themselves together. They have *become one* with wrong things, and it has caused a breach in their souls. Yes, sexual perversion causes a breach in the soul of a man. Subliminal problems persist that cannot be diagnosed. This is a result of crossing illegal lines of sexual behavior. *Chastity, purity,* and *virginity* are rare words in the days we live in. Even in the church, I do not believe that many people have a revelation of how great an effect sexual perversion has on our mental, emotional, and spiritual well-being. Sexual perversion is a yoke that puts a million pounds of weight on the mind. This yoke stems from carnality and ignorance.

THE SPIRIT OF MASTURBATION

It is important to me to begin this teaching by dealing with the spirit of masturbation. My heart was heavy when I found out that a popular preacher was teaching that masturbation was acceptable under certain circumstances. This minister taught that it was all right for the husband to masturbate if his wife maintained a heavy schedule that caused her to be away from him. This minister does not have a revelation of evil imagination. The root of the bondage of masturbation is *evil imagination.* Read Matthew 15:18–19. This passage says that it is what comes from the heart of a man that defiles him—and out of his heart come evil thoughts. Genesis 6:5 tells us that "GOD saw that the wickedness of man was great in the earth, and that every imagination of the thoughts of his heart was only evil continually" (KJV). It was the "imaginations" of men that caused God to flood the earth.

This word *imagination* is *yetser* in Hebrew. It means to continually entertain thoughts that frame the mind. It also means, "to conceive." James 1:15 teaches that when lust is conceived, it brings forth sin. This sin eventually leads to death. As a man continually thinks, he becomes (Prov. 23:7)! Evil imagination builds a frame or stronghold around the mind where lust is conceived. Lust then takes up residence in the mind of the person. Eventually, lustful thoughts give birth to the very acts pondered on. When perversion creeps into a life, the mind of that person is barricaded by a stronghold, which secures darkness. These barriers are reinforced by continual acts of perversion, which build walls higher and higher. These walls ensure that light cannot enter. Where there is no light, there will be heaviness.

In parts of Alaska it is dark for long periods of time. The nights are long and the days are short. During this time of lightlessness, depression and suicide hit record-breaking levels. Sexual promiscuity is a deep, dark bondage that makes the hearts of men heavy.

> **WHEN PERVERSION CREEPS INTO A LIFE, THE MIND OF THAT PERSON IS BARRICADED BY A STRONGHOLD, WHICH SECURES DARKNESS.**

Many people who struggle with perversion also suffer from spirits of depression and suicide. For a few minutes of fleshy gratification, a lifetime of bondage (without the intervention of Jesus Christ) is ignited. Heaviness that persists for long periods of time will definitely bring on deception. A mind that is continually heavy will breed confusion. When a person gets confused, that person's imagination can run wild, causing the person to lose control of reality.

The lyrics of a song made popular by the Motown group The Temptations say: "It was just my imagination running away with me."[1] Though this is a secular song, it is true—*your imagination can run away with you!* It takes strong imagination to masturbate, and it gives room to a bound and blocked spirit. Whenever a person is bound and blocked in his or her own spirit, it opens doors to demon spirits. Spirits never operate alone. Just as ice cream goes with a cake at a birthday party, masturbation goes with pornography, homosexuality, orgies, voyeurism, and many other perverse acts.

THE EVIL INVENTIONS OF MAN

The process of the imagination is rooted in images. Visual images given by books, videos, or the Internet enhance the power of the bondage of the imagination. Telephone sex also enhances the imagination by the sounds that come through the phone. This is a type of witchcraft called *phone voyance*. (You can read about this in my book *Give It Back!*) Once the devil has been given room (access) to the seat of the imagination, the spirit of magnification takes over, and the situation becomes a giant in the land. Many people attempt to make masturbation a small thing. It is an evil giant because it is a type of Baal-peor.

Baal-peor is the "Lord of the opening." This is the name of the deity with whom the children of Israel had affairs in the wilderness. Psalm 106:28–29 says that they joined themselves to Baal-peor and provoked God to anger with their inventions. This one deity opened the doors to many inventions, ideas, abuses, and practices. Because of this, many could not enter the Promised Land.

It is important that we review the term *evil invention*.

1. Psalm 99:8—God avenged the inventions of the children of Israel. This word *invention* is `aliylah, and it indicates a performance of man based on an opportunity to exploit God. In other words, the people of God gave room to the enemy with acts that they created from their own lustful desires.

2. Psalm 106:28–29—The children of Israel joined themselves to Baal-peor, and their inventions provoked the Lord to anger. The word *joined* means to mentally connect oneself to. It meant that the Israelites served this god to the point whereby their minds were framed or caged. They mentally connected to and became one with this demon. The particular word *invention* is ma`alal, and it means to defile by overdoing something. They were spiritually addicted. All perverse acts are rotted in the bondage of habit and addiction. The person bound in the act(s) has a hook in his or her soul, and the enemy has the latch that secures the bondage in place.

3. Ecclesiastes 7:29—This scripture notes that God made man upright, but they strayed by seeking out many inventions. This scripture proves that no person was born in any other nature except heterosexual. The inventions of men perverted them (pulled them off track and into the lie) from the uprightness that God made

them to walk in. This word *invention* is *chishshabown,* and it means to have a mind like a mental engine that produces warfare. Most of the warfare that many struggle with in sexual perversion was manufactured from the wickedness of their own hearts. Proverbs 6:18 refers to a heart that manufactures wickedness.

4. Romans 1:30—This chapter of the Bible calls homosexuals inventors of new forms of evil. This word *inventor* is *epheuretes,* and it relates to a person who contrives or discovers wicked ways of doing things. God did not create man and woman to multiply in the earth realm and then later on bump His head to allow for homosexuality. When a man sexually desires another man, or a woman desires a woman, it is because of something that has been contrived out of the wickedness of their hearts.

Based on the study references above, the hearts of men are wicked from conception. If it can be imagined, it can be invented out of the darkness of our hearts. This is why we need the light of Jesus Christ to shine on the unlit areas of our lives. No one is exempt! Without the transformation of the mind through Jesus Christ, the potential for perversion is in everyone.

The reason I target masturbation so intensely is because it is a strong, idolatrous Baal-peor. It opens the door to deeper bondages. The most important thing to know about it is that there is no such thing as solo sex. When masturbation occurs, the person is opened to the demonic realm. Demons enter in and participate. They infiltrate dream lives and even manifest themselves in the natural. I have prayed for people with physical rape injuries in their bodies from sexual acts committed with demons. I also have a friend who used to be a warlock. He is free today and pastors a small congregation. I will never forget when he explained his initiation to the dark side. He had to make a commitment to be "so-called" celibate for five years. During this five-year demonic consecration, he said that demons visited him in the night and had sex with him. His celibacy was to abstain from having sex with humans. At the time my mind could not fathom a human having sex with a demon. Yet, as I looked into my friend's eyes, I knew he was telling me the truth.

> **WITHOUT THE TRANSFORMATION OF THE MIND THROUGH JESUS CHRIST, THE POTENTIAL FOR PERVERSION IS IN EVERYONE.**

A few years later I was traveling on the road with an elderly mother in the church. She slept at my house because we returned from the trip at a late hour. In the middle of the night, Mother called me into the room where she was sleeping. She was terrified as she explained that a man had come into the room and kissed her on the neck. She was a small, frail woman on kidney dialysis. I could not imagine what she had explained to me. I told her that she had a nightmare, and I assured her that my house is holy.

The next night after I had taken Mother home, I had a strange occurrence as I was sleeping. I was lying on my back, but in my sleep I was lying on my stomach. A huge monster-type figure hovered over the back of my body. It was the foulest, most unclean thing I have ever seen in my life. As it breathed, putrid smoke came out of its mouth, and I remember feeling the breath on my neck. Please excuse my description, but I do not know a better way to express this. The male private part of this creature seemed as big as the room. Do not try to figure it out; the spirit realm is not limited to our understanding of things. This demon tried to attack me sexually but could not because the Lord put a super-natural rubber shield over my body. Nevertheless, the next morning when I got up, I was overwhelmed with a strong feeling of violation.

I cried out to God, "Please, Lord, tell me what that was—because I live a holy life."

The Lord responded by revealing to me that Sherry, a drug addict whom I was allowing to live in my home with me while I was helping her through deliverance, had been entertaining *sex demons*. Sherry denied it with fervency, and I believed her. However, I eventually found out that she had been lying to me.

It was not until later that I remembered Mother's testimony of the man kissing her and my friend's story of having sex with demons as a warlock. I was knocked off my feet, as you may be now if you are hearing something like this for the first time. Do not lean to your own understanding on this one—demons can have sex with people!

The names of the strongmen of these sexual entities are *Incubus* (attacks women sexually) and *Succubus* (attacks men sexually). They usually attack people in their dream lives, but they can manifest in the lives of people while they are awake. As difficult as this may sound, it is biblical. Genesis 6:4 describes how demons came down and had sex with women in the earth, and they gave birth to giants. In the occult world, these demonic births are called *cambiones*. These hideous acts were attributed to the evil imaginations of men. This was one of the main reasons that God flooded the earth. The devil was trying to create an unholy generation and block the coming of the Holy Seed (Jesus). Today, one of the highest sacrifices in the devil-worshiping kingdom is having sex with demons.

It is unholy to spill seed (sperm) on the ground (Gen. 38:9–10). This means to have sex outside of procreation or outside of satisfying your marriage partner. This word *spill* is *shachath,* and it means to corrupt or waste the seed. The word *ground* is *'erets,* and it refers to that which is common or earthly. When we corrupt what God has deemed holy, we become common, which is another word for *worldly* or *unholy.* God commanded the priests to teach the difference between what was *common* and *holy.* (See Leviticus 10:10.) It is my priestly obligation to let you know that sexual intercourse was created by God with a twofold purpose:

1. For the reproduction of mankind as one of the ways to be fruitful and multiply in the earth realm

2. For the intimacy instituted in holy matrimony between a husband (male) and wife (female). Holy matrimony is from God; the institution of marriage is the invention of man. The institution represents "the system"; holy matrimony represents "the spirit."

Anything outside of these two purposes is common, worldly, and unholy. Homosexuality is a lust of the flesh and was created out of the imaginations of men. God was so upset with this invention of man that He repented for creating man. Because of men's evil imaginations, they began to do everything that they imagined to do. Matthew 24:38 says:

> For as in the days before the flood, they were eating and drinking, marrying and giving in marriage, until the day that Noah entered the ark.

The word *marrying* is *gameo* in the Greek, and it means to marry of either sex. They were committing the sin of having same-sex marriages.

It all started with imagination! Same-sex marriage is not some new thing. It was invented out of the wicked hearts of men since the beginning of time. It is an ancient spirit invented out of the wicked hearts of men. The strongman is the lust of the flesh.

LUST

Lust is a bottomless pit, and it is never satisfied. It will always seek new *inventions* to please itself. This is why many famous, handsome, heterosexual men become *down low*, or so-called *bisexual*. I do not believe in bisexuality, because it is not scriptural. What men call *bisexuality* and even *effeminacy* are all forms of homosexuality. God declares in His Word that an effeminate man would not enter the kingdom (1 Cor. 6:9).

Many men dare to claim masculinity after they have had sex with men. Any man who has sex with another man (no matter the position) takes on the role of a woman and should be considered effeminate. Whether a man imagines himself to be a woman, desires to look like a woman, or has sex with another man, he abides in the stronghold of effeminacy and perversion.

I have known many young people who fornicated to the point that they became homosexual. A strong spirit of fornication can open the doors to homosexuality. Atlanta is a stronghold for *down-low brothers*. But this is not due to the unavailability of women, because there are more women than men in Atlanta.[2] Men choose to turn from women to men! Popular young men sleep with so many women they simply got bored, and the demonic influence on their lives causes them to invent something new! The lust demon in them is no longer satisfied and upgrades the level of perversion. One partner is not good enough anymore.

> **LUST IS A BOTTOMLESS PIT, AND IT IS NEVER SATISFIED.**

For many, sodomy becomes the sexual addiction of choice. Eventually the person becomes a *switch-hitter* and can go either way—either a man or a woman will suffice. By this time, many have opened themselves up to orgies, which take them across the lines of what they said they would never do. Other young men and women are seduced into private homosexual relationships through an emotional mess or by the bottomless pits of their own lust.

It is true—as we think, we literally become! All sin is rooted in the imagination. Fornication is the stronghold of all perversion, because its root is in any kind of sexual activity outside of the plan of God. This is why orgies are so big with devil worshipers. They have ceremonies where they conjure spirits to have sex with them. This is considered the highest level of sacrifice in the dark kingdom. Men break their covenant with God and enter into demonic contracts with darkness through sexual perversion.

The spirit realm is made up of roads. Sexual perversion takes a person off the right road and places him or her on the wrong road. Perversion is more a case of *being in a certain place* than it is of *doing an act*. People perform perverted acts because of where they are in the spirit.

The word *pervert* means:

+ To lead off course
+ To bring to a lesser state
+ Mental error or false judgment
+ To twist or misinterpret the truth

Believe it or not, there are levels of perversion. I know that all sin is sin, but all bondage is not on the same level. Perversion is a place that is a deep, dark hole. The longer you stay in it, the deeper you are sucked into it. I have witnessed many who have started with *sexual promiscuity* who eventually have been sucked into debauchery. *Debauchery* is excessive indulgence rooted in sensual pleasure, intemperance, and immorality. If it is not dealt with in time, the person can graduate from a state of debauchery to reprobation. *Reprobation* occurs in a mind that no longer has the ability to serve God and is eternally damned. The first chapter of Romans discusses the progression of people involved in sexual perversion and homosexual sin, which ultimately causes them to be turned over to a reprobate mind.

I know that many may argue that I am taking this thing too far when it comes to sexual sin, but I will not ease up! I love the adulterer, the homosexual, the masturbator, and the fornicator. If it were not for the mercy of God, I would be caught up in the same vicious cycle. But I must highlight the fact that sexual sin is not a problem limited to the world. Our churches also need inner healing from this demon. It gets in the minds of believers and puts a partition between them and God.

On the other hand, it gives room to the devil, and renewal of the mind and a stable relationship with God become impossible. We must wage war against perversion in the church. Our tolerance level has gotten so high for perversion in churches that churches are high on the insurance adjusters' lists for molestation cases. As a result of this, my own church had to purchase expensive extra insurance to cover molestation. It was shocking to me when I was preparing to open my school for children to discover that *all churches are required to carry extra insurance coverage because of the high molestation rate in the body of Christ.*

Also, for the record, I am not *homophobic,* but I am *hell-o-phobic.* At one time in America, preaching against sin was thought to save souls! I hate fornication just as much as homosexuality. The difference between the two is that there is not a group of fornicators fighting to take away my rights as a believer on Capitol Hill. The church must do more than merely *deal with* the homosexual bondage issue—we must spearhead the agenda to do away with sexual perversion!

If you are bound by sexual perversion, I come against all sexual acts that have been created in the caverns of hell and invented in your heart to twist the original plan of God for your life, in the name of Jesus! I command you to be whole and sexually pure. God created sex between one man and one woman so they could be fruitful and manifest His glory in the earth realm. I declare that you are a son (daughter) of God, and you will fall under that order. I pray that you will receive the revelation that the intimacy of marriage is more than an orgasm. Two people becoming one in Christ Jesus in a sanctified marriage cannot be compared to anything the world has invented! I bind homosexuality, adultery, masturbation, fornication, and all other perversions from you. Masturbation and homosexuality are rooted in narcissism. Narcissus fell in love with himself, but you are delivered from self-love. Intimacy in marriage is rooted in the "two becoming one," and not the "one being satisfied"! I speak this over your life, in Jesus's name!

SEXUAL ORIENTATIONS

The sexual orientations listed below can be used in warfare prayer to come against all kinds of lusts and perversions. You may also use this information so that you will not be ignorant of the devices of the enemy. God says that His people perish for a lack of knowledge. The church has been perishing in this area because of ignorance.[3]

1. APOTEMNOPHILIA—sexual arousal associated with the stump(s) of an amputee

2. ASPHYXOPHILIA—sexual gratification derived from activities that involve oxygen deprivation through hanging, strangulation, or other means

3. AUTOGYNEPHILIA—the sexual arousal of a man by his own perception of himself as a woman or dressed as a woman

4. BISEXUAL—the capacity to feel erotic attraction toward, or to engage in sexual interaction with, both males and females

5. COPROPHILIA—sexual arousal associated with feces

6. EXHIBITIONISM—the act of exposing one's genitals to an unwilling observer to obtain sexual gratification

7. FETISHISM/SEXUAL FETISHISM—obtaining sexual excitement primarily or exclusively from an inanimate object or a particular part of the body

8. FROTTEURISM—approaching an unknown woman from the rear and pressing or rubbing the penis against her buttocks

9. HETEROSEXUALITY—the universal norm of sexuality with those of the opposite sex

10. HOMOSEXUAL/GAY/LESBIAN—people who form sexual relationships primarily or exclusively with members of their own gender

11. GENDER IDENTITY DISORDER—a strong and persistent cross-gender identification, which is the desire to be, or the insistence that one is, the other sex, "along with" persistent discomfort about one's assigned sex or a sense of the inappropriateness in the gender role of that sex

12. GERONTOSEXUALITY—distinct preference for sexual relationships primarily or exclusively with an elderly partner

13. INCEST—sex with a sibling or parent

14. KLEPTOPHILIA—obtaining sexual excitement from stealing

15. KLISMAPHILIA—erotic pleasure derived from enemas

16. NECROPHILIA—sexual arousal and/or activity with a corpse

17. PARTIALISM—a fetish in which a person is sexually attracted to a specific body part exclusive of the person

18. PEDOPHILIA—sexual activity with a prepubescent child (generally age thirteen years or younger). The individual with pedophilia must be age sixteen years or older and at least five years older than the child. For individuals in late adolescence with pedophilia, no precise age difference is specified, and clinical judgment must be used; both the sexual maturity of the child and the age difference must be taken into account; the adult may be

sexually attracted to opposite sex, same sex, or prefer either

19. PROSTITUTION—the act or practice of offering sexual stimulation or intercourse for money

20. SEXUAL MASOCHISM—obtaining sexual gratification by being subjected to pain or humiliation

21. SEXUAL SADISM—the intentional infliction of pain or humiliation on another person in order to achieve sexual excitement

22. TELEPHONE SCATALOGIA—sexual arousal associated with making or receiving obscene phone calls

23. TOUCHERISM—characterized by a strong desire to touch the breast or genitals of an unknown woman without her consent; often occurs in conjunction with other paraphilia

24. TRANSGENDERISM—an umbrella term referring to and/or covering transvestitism, drag queen/king, and transsexualism

25. TRANSSEXUAL—a person whose gender identity is different from his or her anatomical gender

26. TRANSVESTITE—a person who is sexually stimulated or gratified by wearing the clothes of the other gender

27. Transvestic Fetishism—intense sexually arousing fantasies, sexual urges, or behaviors involving cross-dressing

28. Urophilia—sexual arousal associated with urine

29. Voyeurism—obtaining sexual arousal by observing people without their consent when they are undressed or engaged in sexual activity

30. Zoophilia/Bestiality—engaging in sexual activity with animals

chapter 13

THE PRIDE OF LIFE

PASSAGE OF SCRIPTURE in 1 John reveals that the love of the world will give room to the pride of life.

> Do not love the world or the things in the world. If anyone loves the world, the love of the Father is not in him. For all that is in the world—the lust of the flesh, the lust of the eyes, and the pride of life—is not of the Father but is of the world.
> —1 John 2:15–16

It is impossible to love the world and love God at the same time. The Bible says we will hate one and love the other. God abides so far away from worldliness that our reach is not long enough to hold on to the world and have Him too. He is holy! By clinging to the things of the world, men receive the fruit of the world, which are:

+ The lust of the eyes
+ The lust of the flesh
+ The pride of life

I am convinced that many people struggle in life because of the spirit of pride. The definition of *pride* is "to have a high opinion of one's own dignity, importance, and superiority." It is dangerous to have self-esteem or self-respect that is too high. Romans 12:3 warns us not to think more of ourselves than we ought to. Scripture proves that the spirit of pride is often associated with the rejection of God. Whether a person is aware of being rejected by God or not, rejection from God releases a dark cloud. A person who has been rejected by God can have an abundance of things in his or her life but still feel that something will always be missing. That person will have an empty space in the heart that was reserved for God alone.

It may be hard for many to imagine that God would reject anyone. This sounds nice, but it is a religious mind-set. Surely it is not scriptural. Below are seven scriptures that support the fact that God does reject people.

> He has shown strength and made might with His arm; He has scattered the proud and haughty in and by the imagination and purpose and designs of their hearts.
>
> —Luke 1:51, AMP

> But He gives us more and more grace (power of the Holy Spirit, to meet this evil tendency and all others fully). That is why He says, God sets Himself against the proud and haughty, but gives grace [continually] to the lowly (those who are humble enough to receive it).
>
> —James 4:6, AMP

> Likewise, you who are younger and of lesser rank, be subject to the elders (the ministers and spiritual guides of the church)—[giving them due respect and yielding to their counsel]. Clothe (apron) yourselves, all of you, with humility [as the garb of a servant, so that its covering cannot possibly be stripped from you, with freedom from pride and arrogance] toward one another. For God sets Himself against the proud (the insolent, the overbearing, the disdainful, the presumptuous, the boastful)—[and He opposes, frustrates, and defeats them], but gives grace (favor, blessing) to the humble.
>
> —1 Peter 5:5, AMP

From the wicked their light is withheld, and their uplifted arm
is broken.
—Job 38:15, AMP

Rise up, O Judge of the earth; render to the proud a fit compen-
sation!
—Psalm 94:2, AMP

You rebuke the proud and arrogant, the accursed ones, who err
and wander from Your commandments.
—Psalm 119:21, AMP

For there shall be a day of the Lord of hosts against all who are
proud and haughty and against all who are lifted up—and they
shall be brought low.
—Isaiah 2:12, AMP

Only a person with a proud spirit would deny that the proud are
rejected by God. God loves all men, but no flesh will glory in His
sight. The spirit of pride separates us from God. Job 41:15 says that
Leviathan's (the king of the children of pride) scales are his pride. The
scales are so closely sealed together that no air can get in. This word
air is *ruwach*, which means breath of God. Where the breath of God
cannot get in, there will be no revival. People are being asphyxiated by
life challenges. They need to be revived, and it can only happen by the
breath of God. Pride stands in the doorways of their hearts and minds,
and revival is shut down in their lives. For too long churches have had
revivals in buildings made of brick and stone. Men need revival in their
hearts and minds. This begins the inner healing process.

Many people are too proud to deal with issues they have carried
in their hearts for years. These things linger and deny access to God.
As the scriptures reveal, He is close to those with a contrite spirit and

saves the ones with a broken heart. A proud heart and a haughty spirit cannot receive the wind of God's inner healing. There are demonic strongmen that hide behind prideful hearts. What people tend to call a *strong will* is really a *stronghold* for demons to rule over souls.

> **MEN NEED REVIVAL IN THEIR HEARTS AND MINDS. THIS BEGINS THE INNER HEALING PROCESS.**

THE STRONGMEN OF PRIDE

Leviathan is the king of the children of pride, and he takes second to none. The scales on his back are his pride. Most strongmen cover the demons that support them, but this is not so with Leviathan. Leviathan is covered by scales (demons) under which he hides and operates discreetly. Job 41:15 describes the scales of pride on Leviathan's back. The Amplified Version of the Bible says that they are like rows of shields. There is a Hebrew word for *scales, qasqeseth,* and it relates to a coat of mail covered with joining plates. (See Leviticus 11:9, "scales.") This Hebrew word is the same word for the coat of mail that Goliath wore.

Goliath is also a type of strongman. Its power is perfected in spirits of magnification and mockery. Goliath is the spirit that makes a lot of threats but cannot stand up against the power of God. Both of these strongmen (Goliath and Leviathan) hide under the covering of smaller imps. Their covering is the *qasqeseth,* the strong plates that join to form a coat of mail on their backs.

This is how the spirit of *qasqeseth* works. A person who is actually trapped in a stronghold of pride may only manifest bitterness and rejection, but the spirit of pride is the root problem. It hides behind the scenes. The two smaller demons (bitterness and rejection) are the *qasqeseth* or distracting decoys that cover the strongman of pride. The Bible clearly states that if the strongman is not dealt with, we cannot get what is in his house. The two smaller demons in this case are distractions from the root problem. While a minister may be targeting the spirits of bitterness and rejection, pride comfortably hides behind the scenes. As I have mentioned throughout this book, inner healing deals with the roots.

> For the weapons of our warfare are not physical [weapons of flesh and blood], but they are mighty before God for the overthrow and destruction of strongholds, [Inasmuch as we] refute arguments and theories and reasonings and every proud and lofty thing that sets itself up against the [true] knowledge of God; and we lead every thought and purpose away captive into the obedience of Christ (the Messiah, the Anointed One), Being in readiness to punish every [insubordinate for his] disobedience, when your own submission and obedience [as a church] are fully secured and complete.
> —2 Corinthians 10:4–6, AMP

Job 41:34 says that Leviathan beholds all high things. A person with a haughty spirit is subject to the rules of the kingdom of Leviathan; he is their king! Pride parades itself before destruction, and a haughty spirit is the precursor to a fall. Pride and haughtiness promote failure. Failure always depresses the soul, because God created mankind to have dominion. This dominion is not limited to believers only, but it is for all of mankind. This is why unbelievers can operate in power outside of the power of God. It is because of the dominion of mankind, a false power or false prosperity that deceives men into relaxing in the achievements of the world without God.

Many people who do not have God in their lives are bound by the pride of life. They depend on their own strength to be successful in life. This in itself makes it easy to see why there are so many depressed, suicidal people in the world. Attempting to be an achiever in this world, without the help of the One who created it, weighs heavy on the soul. Leviathan beholds (holds a watch over) the high-minded. (See Job 41.) Second Corinthians 10 speaks of the high thing that exalts itself above the true knowledge of God (v. 5). The enemy tricks the proud in heart to hold themselves in a place higher than God. In the natural, men cannot breathe at certain altitudes. The higher they are, the less oxygen they have. The high-minded are cut off from the breath (*ruwach*) of God. Failure is inevitable. In 2 Corinthians 10:5, the Greek word for *high thing* is *hupsoma*, and it references "that which has elevated self." There is no medication to deliver a person from a high place to which he has elevated himself.

The only way to get out of the stronghold of the high place is through humility. I would like to bring attention to two Greek words for humility:

1. *Tapeinos*—to lower self to the floor (James 4:6, "humble")

2. *Tapeinophrosune*—humility unto humiliation (Acts 20:19, "humility")

To get a revelation of these definitions of humility allows one to understand why pride is such a stronghold. Who is willing to humble themselves to the floor? Who will submit to the humiliation that God will cause to come upon a person to save his or her soul?

During this past year several leaders of major ministries have been exposed with sin in their lives. We all fall short of the glory of God, and in no way do I come up against their falling. But I do have a problem with the ones who continue to put on a show in the midst of their humiliation. When God causes humiliation, the best thing that we can do is lower ourselves to the floor.

> **THE ENEMY TRICKS THE PROUD IN HEART TO HOLD THEMSELVES IN A PLACE HIGHER THAN GOD.**

One particular minister was caught in a humiliating situation. The minister's response was to entertain people (worldwide) by telling them that the situation was that person's destiny. This is the wrong answer! The humiliating situation was not the minister's destiny—it was an opportunity to get down to the floor. The answer to this minister's situation would have been to bow and be humbled under the mighty hand of God. God will exalt a person in due season, if it is His will. Self-exaltation is demonic. It is oppressive when people attempt to exalt themselves in the midst of a mess. They only dig themselves into a hole that is deeper than what they were already in.

Isaiah 27:1 (KJV) calls Leviathan "that crooked serpent." He is also referred to as "the piercing serpent." The term *piercing* means fugitive spirit. Leviathan hides in the lives of individuals to make them unstable. This spirit causes people to run from place to place like vagabonds. It also causes them to never finish things. They have many loose ends and uncompleted things in their lives. They are cursed to have no completion.

The crooked serpent gives people the inability to walk straight. It is a winding spirit that keeps men walking in circles, making wrong decisions and being led in the wrong direction. The crooked serpent also breeds error and deception. It is the underlying force that locks in the backsliding spirit. Even when a person thinks of coming back to God, the crooked serpent secures his steps in an opposite direction. Though Leviathan is the chief ruling spirit of pride, this spirit walks hand in hand with two other spirits to form a threefold cord that will ensure a fall.

THE DEMONIC THREEFOLD CORD OF PRIDE

Leviathan (Neck)	Behemoth (Loins)	Cockatrice (Mind)

Notice that each spirit lodges itself in a particular part of the body. The place where they are lodged is where their strength lies. As we mentioned earlier, Leviathan's strength is in the neck. I believe that this is because the yoke of bondage is seated in the neck.

> It shall come to pass in that day
> That his burden will be taken away from your shoulder,
> And his *yoke from your neck*,
> And the yoke will be destroyed because of the anointing oil
> —Isaiah 10:27, emphasis added

Behemoth's strength abides in the loins. (See Job 40:16.) This is a spirit of deception. This is a sign of great deception when a hippopotamus thinks that he is a greyhound. A hippo is a large sloppy creature, and a greyhound is slim and trim. The behemoth causes its victim to think totally opposite of the truth. The spirit of the behemoth takes a person into a fantasy world of deception. They never realize the bondage until it is too late.

> Indeed the river may rage,
> Yet he is not disturbed;

He is confident, though the Jordan gushes into his mouth,
Though he takes it in his eyes,
Or one pierces his nose with a snare.
—Job 40:23–24

It is clear that the behemoth is a gluttonous spirit that takes in more than it can handle. The behemoth's eyes are bigger than his belly. He is so confident that he has no fear. He does not tremble! The behemoth is the spirit that gets in the loins of a man and causes him not to fear God.

God had to deal with the pride that got into Job's loins in Job 40. At the beginning of the chapter, Job contended with God. He questioned the way that God was handling things in his life. God was so angry with Job that He got on the inside of a whirlwind to speak to him. I believe that if God had not gotten into the whirlwind, Job would have died when God spoke to him. God warned Job to gird up his loins like a man (v. 7, KJV). When it comes to girding our loins, it must be done with truth. Job had the deception of the behemoth in his loins.

A lie is an upfront enemy of truth, but deception lurks behind the scenes and operates unnoticed. Job was deceived into responding to God as though he was on the same level as God. Job contended with and attempted to instruct God (v. 2, KJV). The word *contend* is *riyb* in the Hebrew language, and it means:

+ To defend one's self against God
+ To complain
+ To question and debate
+ To rebuke and correct

What great deception! Can you imagine Job trying to correct God? It was as though Job thought that God did not know how to rule over his life. God had to draw a line and remind Job of His majesty. God reminded Job that He was the God of Creation. He also made a very interesting offer to Job. Since Job questioned the manner of the Almighty's rule, God challenged him to put on majesty and rule the world. God also bid Job to look on everyone who was proud and make them abase (or cause them to become humble). He went further by telling Job to bury and hide the proud in the dust and shut them up in hell. I believe that God used the example of the proud because it is a spirit that only God Himself can deal with. Pride demands lordship.

Throughout the fortieth and forty-first chapters of Job, God described the creatures (the behemoth and Leviathan) that He created and how powerful they are. God asked who can deal with these creatures in their might. Then He reminded Job that He created them and gave them the power that they have. This is to cause Job—and us—to bring the question to mind: If God is the Creator of these powerful creatures, who would have the nerve to challenge God?

God takes offense when we think that we know how to run our lives better than He does. When He says that all things will work out for our good, He means just that! Spirits of pride and rebellion rule the hearts of men, and these people are held back in life because they have not accepted God's way for them. Many pray for the will of God to be done in their lives, but they do not give in to the ways of God. God not only has a *will* to do things in our lives, but He also has the *way* He wants to use to accomplish His will.

Healing cannot get into the depths of our souls until we *let go and let God!* We must have a reverential fear of God to have abundant life.

As I studied the Scriptures, it was revealed to me how God's voice can be like thunder (Job 40:9). When I was a little girl, old people would make us sit down and be quiet when it thundered. Some of them were not even saved. Though this act was passed down through generations, I did not understand what was really at the root of it.

> **HEALING CANNOT GET INTO THE DEPTHS OF OUR SOULS UNTIL WE LET GO AND LET GOD!**

I did know that at Mount Sinai, when the people tried to hear from God they ran away holding their ears. They could not stand the thunder of God's voice, and they begged Moses to go before God for them. How many times have we ignored thunder? I believe that thunder is the voice of God. He does not always speak this way, but when He does, we need to be still and listen. When we ignore the thunder of God's voice, we do not fear Him.

The spirit of behemoth makes people overconfident, and the lack of the fear of God sets in. They begin to dabble in sin because they are confident that they can handle it. King Solomon's loins were gripped by the behemoth. (See 1 Kings 11:1–11.) God warned him not to get involved with foreign women. He ended up with one thousand wives and concubines. Solomon thought he had these women, when in reality they had him. The deception drove him to worshiping other gods.

Leviathan and the behemoth flow together demonically. Pride and deception come together to blind the mind. This is where the cockatrice comes into play. It is a mind-blinding spirit. The cockatrice is described as a mythological creature in the dictionary. Since several scriptures in the Bible refer to the cockatrice, I beg to differ with this point. Although it must be spiritually discerned, the cockatrice really exists. Let's review the scriptures.

And the sucking child shall play over the hole of the asp, and the weaned child shall put his hand on the adder's den.

—Isaiah 11:8, AMP

Rejoice not, O Philistia, all of you, because the rod [of Judah] that smote you is broken; for out of the serpent's root shall come forth an adder [King Hezekiah of Judah], and its [the serpent's] offspring will be a fiery, flying serpent.

—Isaiah 14:29, AMP

They hatch adders' eggs and weave the spider's web; he who eats of their eggs dies, and [from an egg] which is crushed a viper breaks out [for their nature is ruinous, deadly, evil]. Their webs will not serve as clothing, nor will they cover themselves with what they make; their works are works of iniquity, and the act of violence is in their hands.

—Isaiah 59:5–6, AMP

A mind-blinding spirit causes total confusion in the mind of a person. Often I have dealt with cases whereby the conversations of the person made no sense. The person continually repeated the same thing over and over again. Trying to get a point over to that person was impossible. When confusion has lodged itself in the mind of a person, you must deal with the threefold cord of pride. Deal with the bondage in the neck, the loins, and the mind. Sever the agreement of the strongmen by breaking any cords between them, and cast them out of the person. Deal with each spirit individually. Start with Leviathan because he holds the yoke in place. Then deal with the deception in the loins, and the cockatrice will have to retreat and leave.

Satan is the god of this world. He roots himself in the pride of life. The devil hides behind false success. What is false success? It is success without God. Do not be deceived to think that you are so holy that the devil will not tempt you. He tempted Jesus in the wilderness. He used the threefold cord of temptation:

+ Power ("Command these stones to be made into bread")
+ Fame ("Son of God, cast Thyself down")
+ Mammon ("All these things will I give thee")

Even if a person is suffering from emotional or mental disturbances in his or her life, deal with the spirit of pride first. It is the root of many problems. A spirit of pride may have grown up with a person, or a demon may have entered through a traumatic experience. Pride will even stop a person from dealing with the spirit of pride. Coming against pride can never hurt in a counseling or deliverance session. Listed below are the fruits of a prideful heart. Call them out, and deal with them as they manifest. God may also reveal other things that need to be dealt with, which you can add to your list.

1. Lofty self-respect
2. Self-satisfaction
3. Self-importance
4. An overbearing spirit
5. Disdain
6. An imperious attitude
7. Presumption
8. Arrogance
9. A haughty spirit
10. A zealous preservation of one's dignity
11. An affectionate admiration of things that pertain to self
12. Extreme selfishness
13. Exaggerated faith in self
14. To be swollen or puffed up

A PROUD BOASTER

Proverbs 6:17 tells us that one of the seven things that God hates is a proud look. I do not believe that it is necessarily the look that God hates, but it is what is behind the look that He does not like. A haughty spirit is a type of pride that flaunts itself. This kind of pride does not care what anyone thinks about it. A haughty or proud look will eventually promote itself to boasting. Boasting can be godly or ungodly. Paul declared that his boast was in the Lord (2 Cor. 10:13). He bragged about the great things that God had done and did not neglect to give Him the glory. God loves when we boast in Him. It is good to boast as long as the credit is pointed toward God.

There is also godly and ungodly pride. Pride and the spirit of boasting are twin friends. They walk hand in hand and always complement each other. A good way to discern the spirit of pride is through a boastful conversation. An ungodly proud spirit will manifest itself in the life of a person through the *spirit of boasting*. As I was doing a word search on boasting, I found three Greek words that explain it all:

1. *Kauchaomai*—to glory (see 2 Corinthians 10:13, "boast")

2. *Kauchema*—the actual boasting (see Romans 4:2, "to glory")

3. *Kauchesis*—the act of boasting (see Romans 3:27, "boasting")

All three of these words come from one Greek word, *auchen*, which means neck.[1] It is described as one who stretches the neck and holds it in the position of pride. This is how the proud look sets in. Even when the person is not trying to be proud, his or her neck is stuck in the position of pride. The definition of *auchen* also refers to pride that causes the person to think they have made themselves. It is a sin to even think we have made ourselves in any arena in life.

> When you have eaten and are full, then you shall bless the LORD your God for the good land which He has given you. Beware that you do not forget the LORD your God by not keeping His commandments, His judgments, and His statutes which I command you today, lest—when you have eaten and are full, and have built beautiful houses and dwell in them; and when your herds and your flocks multiply, and your silver and your gold are multiplied, and all that you have is multiplied; when your heart is lifted up, and you forget the LORD your God who brought you out of the land of Egypt, from the house of bondage; who led you through that great and terrible wilderness, in which were fiery serpents and scorpions and thirsty land where there was no water; who brought water for you out of the flinty rock; who fed you in the wilderness with manna, which your fathers did not know, that He might humble you and that He might test you, to do you good in the end—then you say in your heart, *"My power and the might of my hand have gained me this wealth."* And you shall remember the LORD your God, for it is He who gives you power to get wealth, that He may establish His covenant which He swore to your fathers, as it is this day. Then it shall be, if you by any means forget the LORD your God, and follow other gods, and serve them and worship them, I testify against you this day that you shall surely perish. As the nations which the LORD destroys before you, so you shall perish, because you would not be obedient to the voice of the LORD your God.
>
> —Deuteronomy 8:10–20, emphasis added

In the passage of Scripture above, we can see how *kauchaomai* fits into the picture. It is a glory-snatching spirit that attempts to take God's credit. A proud boaster has a spirit that shows off. The Greek word for this is *huperephanos,* and it means *huper* (over) *phanos* (to show off)—to show off excessively. (See Romans 1:30, "proud.")

The perfect example of a *show-off spirit* is addressed in the eighth chapter of Deuteronomy. God warns His people that after He blesses them, they need to remember Him. When we remember God and what He has brought us out of, there is no room for showing off. Many live today believing that their jobs, gifts, families, or ministries have gotten them wealth. God fed His people with manna to humble and test them. But even then, some of the Israelites just didn't get it. They didn't understand that the purpose for the day-to-day provision was *to keep them humble* when they got into the land of milk and honey. What does it prosper a man to gain the entire world and lose his soul to pride?

I have been blessed to minister to some of the richest people in the world. God has taken me into arenas with the greatest athletes and biggest movie stars. I have eaten dinner with kings and fellowshiped with world leaders. The situation is the same everywhere I go. People are miserable without God. People who have everything accessible to them in life are still depressed, suicidal, and live their lives under a dark cloud that rains on them daily. I am convinced that most of them forgot who gave them the power to get wealth. I believe that as we grow financially and materially, we must grow spiritually. This is what *zoe* life is all about. I spoke of *zoe* life in an earlier chapter. Now I would like to compare it to *bios* life.

ZOE LIFE VS. BIOS LIFE

I believe that the greatest key for unlocking the door to inner healing is having a revelation of *zoe* life. *Zoe* is the life that God gives! Jesus said that He came that we might have abundant life (*zoe*). *Zoe* life exists without end and operates in opposition to death. The opposite of *zoe* life is *bios* life. *Bios* life is simply life without *zoe* or life without God. The Greek word *bios* is related to the word *biology*, which is the scientific study of life. Our world is plagued with so-called great minds that have figured out life scientifically. I thank God for science, but to many, modern-day science is their god. We need biological life to connect to the earth, but the problem sets in when life according to science rules over life according to God. If the world could get this revelation, our mental hospitals would have fewer occupants.

We live in a world where knowledge is god. The religion Scientology is growing rapidly in the world. It is especially growing where the rich and famous preside. I have counseled with many in Hollywood who have paid (double-digit) thousands of dollars to have abundant life through Scientology.

> **I BELIEVE THAT THE GREATEST KEY FOR UNLOCKING THE DOOR TO INNER HEALING IS HAVING A REVELATION OF *ZOE* LIFE.**

For example, it takes a minimum of $50,000 to be (what they call) *flattened*. This is a process whereby members of this group are deadened to emotions that affect them because of things from their past. This group also emphasizes knowledge to the point that members are encouraged to know the definitions of as many words as they can. They carry dictionaries around like Bibles. They handle their everyday situations by defining words that relate to their problems. For instance, if a wife says something to a husband that offends him, he will look up a word that is related to their situation, and they both discuss it. They get understanding from the meaning of the word, and from that aspect settle their issue. This is twisted truth! They should not seek counsel from words but from the Word of God. It is the only thing that sets men free.

Another deception of Scientology is the participation of marriage partners in agreed infidelity. I have talked to some who even swap spouses. Based on what I was told by a member of the group, it is acceptable for a spouse to sleep with someone outside the marriage if the other spouse agrees with it. This is a great example of *bios* life. It is life that is not subject to the laws of God. We live in a day where people want religious activity without a relationship with God. They want to live good lives that make them feel better. The truth of the matter is that no one feels better when they are living in outright rebellion against God. Outside of the laws of God, there is no peace, no joy, and only emptiness.

In the world of the rich and the famous, everyone has a therapist. People spend thousands of dollars seeking the counsel of men to make their lives better. The counsel they receive makes sin a social choice and God a bore. First John 2:16 speaks of the pride of life. *Alazoneia ho bios* means "pride of life." It relates to:

+ Ambition
+ Vain, glorious pursuit of honors
+ A show-off spirit
+ The splendor of life
+ The luxury of life

All of these things lead to depression and misery. They force people to live double lives because of the shame of who they really are. The

Greek word *kenodoxia* is a type of pride whereby people pretend to be what they are not. (See Philippians 2:3, "vainglory.") *Huperephania* is another Greek word for pride, and it relates to a type of pride that is encompassed in the desire to show off what one has in comparison to others, thus appearing above them. (See Mark 7:22.) In laymen's terms, it is the "keeping up with the Joneses" spirit.

I am convinced that many people would not suffer from emotional distress from life challenges if they would accept who God made them to be and how He wants to run their lives. My motto in life is that I do not compare what God has for me to what He has for anyone else. I refuse to compete with anyone. I choose to maintain my confidence in God in my marriage, ministry, family, and all other areas of my life. My competition is against my own flesh. I believe in consistent increase in God as He takes me level to level. Every year of my life I celebrate victory as I beat myself (do better) as life moves on. Daily, I rejoice in the fact that I may not be where I want to be, but I am where I need to be and definitely not where I used to be. I am always closer to my mark, doing better than I did! When I rise early to command my mornings, I can look into the mirror and say to my flesh, "You lost again, because my spirit beat you out." I can make it to the next day.

> Keep awake and watch and pray [constantly], that you may not enter into temptation; the spirit indeed is willing, but the flesh is weak
>
> —Mark 14:38, AMP

> Do you not know that in a race all the runners compete, but [only] one receives the prize? So run [your race] that you may lay hold [of the prize] and make it yours. Now every athlete who goes into training conducts himself temperately and restricts himself in all things. They do it to win a wreath that will soon

wither, but we [do it to receive a crown of eternal blessedness] that cannot wither. Therefore I do not run uncertainly (without definite aim). I do not box like one beating the air and striking without an adversary. But [like a boxer] I buffet my body [handle it roughly, discipline it by hardships] and subdue it, for fear that after proclaiming to others the Gospel and things pertaining to it, I myself should become unfit [not stand the test, be unapproved and rejected as a counterfeit].

—1 Corinthians 9:24–27, AMP

This is what life on earth is all about, running your own race! My prayer is that your spirit will win in the end, and you will stand before God to receive the only prize that counts—eternal life in Jesus Christ.

chapter 14

GOD HEALS!

D R. Martin Luther King Jr. was quoted as saying that a person had not really lived until they found something that they were willing to die for. This chapter is dedicated to a few people who "loved not their lives unto the death" (Rev. 12:11, KJV). Their testimonies qualify them as spiritual martyrs according to Revelation 12.

> And they have overcome (conquered) him by means of the blood of the Lamb and by the utterance of their testimony, for they did not love and cling to life even when faced with death [holding their lives cheap till they had to die for their witnessing]. Therefore be glad (exult), O heavens and you that dwell in them! But woe to you, O earth and sea, for the devil has come down to you in fierce anger (fury), because he knows that he has [only] a short time [left]!
> —Revelation 12:11–12, AMP

The word *testimony* in this passage means to be a martyr or to die for what you believe in. It is easy to seek that which is worth living for, but few seek things in life that are worth dying for. I thank God for the stories of the four people highlighted in this chapter. They had to die to shame to allow me to tell their stories. These stories all lead to victory and shed light on the fact that God heals no matter how deep and dark a situation may be.

This chapter is full of victory, and the devil is overcome by the words of these testimonies. It is no secret that you are about to read testimonies of people who have been through something. They have been delivered from what they have been through and have proof in their lives that they are not going back. This is the evidence that manifests itself against the lies of the devil and the world to let men know that Jesus really heals!

Revelation 12:12 lets us know that the devil is already mad. He was mad when he hit the ground. When a powerful testimony of deliverance is given, the devil has something to (really) be mad about! Though my testimony is my ministry, my ministry is not limited to testimony. I am also charged to have a sound word that will equip and train the saints. I do rejoice in the fact that the devil hates testimonies, especially the ones that keep things real. So many people are wondering if God really heals. Does He heal bodies, does He heal hearts, and does He heal minds? This chapter is a witness in the earth realm that *GOD HEALS*! He even heals people with hard cases in hard places.

The earth is surrounded by a cloud of witnesses who have died for the gospel of Jesus Christ—for real! They were crucified upside down, stoned, burned alive, and boiled in oil. Today few people become martyrs to this extent. But there are still martyrs, and the least we can do is to…TELL IT! It will only cost us a little pride. I thank God for the martyrs who testified in this chapter. I know that their faithfulness and dedication will bring healing to many lives. I believe testimonies seal inner healing. When we can tell what we have come out of, it soothes the soul. We do not have to live in dark closets or walk around with things held over our heads.

When we fear talking about the issues in our lives (when God has prompted us to testify), it may be because there has been no healing. I know that testimonies must be subjected to the timing of God, but they can be extremely liberating when they are Spirit-led.

God did not just give His Word to us in a subliminal form, forcing us to try to figure it out in the Bible. He gave stories and testimonies of people who really lived. The people mentioned in the Bible had real problems that were dealt with by a real God—One who *heals!* I pray that the following testimonies will bless you and cause a domino effect of deliverance and healing to be your portion. Enjoy!

MARY

I know a young woman who was a military dependent wife with three children at the time of her transition in life. She was living a double life behind the scenes. She had been addicted to crack cocaine for ten years and often turned to prostitution to support her habit. Her husband was consistently stationed in other countries. Mary* had a beautiful, four-bedroom home in a very nice neighborhood, cars, nice furniture, and all the accessories of life that caused people to think she was stable. Her husband never knew that the wife and mother of his three children was addicted to crack and was a woman of the streets.

Eventually, the curtains of this lifestyle were pulled open as instance after instance began to occur in Mary's life. Her life began to spiral

---

* Not her real name

downward as she went to a neighborhood on the north side of Jackson-ville, Florida, to purchase crack cocaine. One night she made a drug purchase in the midst of an undercover stakeout. The officers pulled her and the man she was with over immediately after purchasing the drugs. She was handcuffed and laid in the street with all the other people who were arrested that night.

Mary was incarcerated in jail for two days. After obtaining legal counsel, it was determined that she had been arrested illegally, and all of the charges were dropped. A few years later, Mary had another close call. She gave some guys a ride to a store. Mary waited in the car for the guys as they entered the store. Minutes later the guys came running out of the store, shooting as they jumped into the car. When they demanded Mary to drive off, she realized that she was involved in an actual robbery. No one was harmed during the incident that night. Mary got away from the robbers safely and began to dread the things she had come into contact with.

Close call after close call like these began to weigh heavily on Mary's soul, and she became suicidal. She so desired to be free from her addiction, but she felt as if she had no way out. She experienced uncontrollable urges to end her life every week. The icing was placed on the cake when Mary had a very long drug binge. She had been using crack for days at a time. At the end of her ordeal she found herself unable to control her bodily fluids. She was vomiting profusely and actually felt as though she was at death's door.

After a short stay in the city hospital, Mary took a break from the streets. She started attending a church, but immediately after every service she went to the bar across the street from the church and purchased liquor and cigarettes. She was in church but not of the church. Something was still missing in her life!

One day Mary went to a beauty salon to get her hair done. There was a woman in the salon talking about Jesus. The woman was loud and so bold about what she was saying that Mary was impressed to follow her outside when she left. The woman ministered to Mary and gave her a prophetic word. That night, on a sidewalk in the front of a salon, Mary gave her heart to the Lord and received the baptism of the Holy Spirit.

After this experience, Mary tried to go back to her life of drugs and darkness, but God had a grip in her soul. The woman gave Mary her personal contact information, and after another attempt to use drugs, Mary ran to the woman's house with her three children. Mary was given a place to dry out from the drugs, and the woman watched her children. Mary became a full-time member of this woman's church. They did spiritual warfare and had a ministry of casting of demons. They were even called the *Demon Busters*.

Yes, I was the woman whom Mary ran into that day at the salon. The night that Mary was lying on the streets during the drug bust, she was at a house in front of Spoken Word Ministries where I am the pastor. The man in the car with Mary that night was also supernaturally delivered and is now an ordained minister at Spoken Word Ministries. God's plan for Mary was working behind the scenes while the devil thought he had her.

After joining the church, Mary continued to have challenges in life. But to God's glory, she was drug free and living for the Lord! The seeds of the past grew into bad fruit in Mary's marriage, and eventually her husband left her for another woman. At this time Mary was ready to be a godly wife and mother, but her husband declared it was too late. Financial difficulties became a major hindrance in her life. Her divorce settlement was bitter and hostile, and Mary lost custody of her children as a result. Despite the life challenges that Mary experienced, she continued to allow Jesus to be the center of her joy.

Today Mary has a flourishing career in the military. She is also involved in international athletic competitions in the military. Total restoration has been made with her children, and she is happily living as a single mother. She is an ordained prophet and has traveled around the world with me. Mary preaches the gospel of Jesus Christ with revelation and power and testifies that the things she has come out of are a strong foundation. The healing that God has given her has blessed her and her future generations. She does not suffer from fear, depression, or the tormenting spirits that once controlled her life. Jesus controls her, spiritually, mentally, emotionally, physically, and financially. Mary rejoices that she has been made a whole woman.

> **GOD'S PLAN FOR MARY WAS WORKING BEHIND THE SCENES WHILE THE DEVIL THOUGHT HE HAD HER.**

ARDELL DANIELS (MY HUSBAND)

Ardell Daniels was born fifty years ago to Florzell and Odessa Daniels. When he was eight months old, his father left his mother and three other siblings and moved around the corner from their house to start another family. Eventually his father left the city, never to be heard of again until Ardell met him at the age of twenty-one. Because he was only eight months old when his father left, he had no recollection of his father.

Ardell was raised by his grandfather and grandmother, Pleas and Daisy Daniels, in Belle Glade, Florida. Daisy Daniels is still alive today in Belle Glade, Florida, and celebrated her one hundredth birthday on September 29, 2007. Pleas Daniels was a sharecropper born in Blakely, Georgia. He moved to Florida because he always came out in the red at the end of each year's crop. Pleas moved to Belle Glade and made a living for his family working in the fields with the migrant workers.

Ardell began to do his part to support the family's economic survival at an early age. His responsibility was to get up at 3:30 a.m. every morning to wake up other family members on the property who worked in the fields. Just four years old at the time, he had to walk half a mile at 3:30 a.m. each morning. By the age of five, Ardell worked in the fields of Belle Glade also. His family never lived in a house of their own until he was six years old. Before that, they lived in a shelter made with tin walls. Bedsheets separated each room on the inside to provide walls. Up to seven people lived in the four-hundred-square-foot tin shelter, which often exposed the family to the elements. Trucks from the fields came often to the area filled with the tin shelters housing the migrant workers so they could pick up the food from the ground as they pleased.

By the time Ardell was in his early teens, he remembers staying out as late as he desired. His grandfather's only rule was that he arose at 3:30 a.m. to work in the fields. Ardell grew up hanging out in a place in Belle Glade called Raiderville. This was an area of town dedicated to gambling, prostitution, and drug crime. In the fields he was exposed to crop planes dropping off drugs as they fled the border patrol police.

The young people of Belle Glade were conditioned to believe that their destiny was rooted in three choices: working in the fields, getting an athletic scholarship, or becoming a drug dealer. Today Belle Glade, Florida, is known for releasing some of the greatest athletes in the world. Though he never pursued it, Ardell received a full basketball scholarship to the University of Kansas. Instead, at the age of eighteen he took $1,000 worth of marijuana to Tallahassee, Florida, and enrolled at Florida A&M University. He became a student drug dealer upon arrival. Ardell often used his financial aid money to restock his marijuana supply. Finally he gave up the pursuit of a college degree with only a few hours left to graduate.

Later Ardell became a city bus driver and drove through the campus of Florida A&M University as a cover for his drug business. Ardell had several relationships with women and managed more than one household. I was one of those women.[1]

After a temporary breakup with me, Ardell married another woman and pursued a legal career in the air conditioning business. He obtained a certified contractor's license with the State of Florida in 1992. Ardell testifies that out of two thousand people taking the test, he was one of two African Americans in the room. With this test having only a 30 percent passing ratio, Ardell was one of the participants who received a license. The ironic thing is that he was still high on crack cocaine when he took the test, having done drugs for twenty-four hours straight before taking the test.

Ardell was what he calls a *functional junkie*. He was desperately addicted to drugs but maintained a legitimate occupation. He tells stories of doing crack with surgeons before they went into the operating room, teachers before they went to their classes in their high schools, and judges before they judged cases. He started his own air conditioning company with up to twenty-five employees at one time. Ardell remembers the times that he gave his employees paychecks and took the checks back immediately by selling them drugs.

The lines of the Spirit fell on Ardell Daniels as we reconnected. He gave his life to the Lord and began to fulfill the call of God on his life. Ardell, known to many as Danny, made a choice when he met me. He followed me as I have followed Jesus. Today I am his pastor, wife, the mother of his identical twins (Elijah and Elisha), and his best friend. That day Ardell ran across me (after fourteen years since we last saw each other), he was detoured from a drug deal. This deal took some of his friends and associates in the drug world into a court case that cost some of them a double-life prison sentence. Ardell ministers to some of these guys doing time in prison today.

> **THE STRENGTH OF HIS DELIVERANCE FROM THE POVERTY, BONDAGE, AND PERVERSION OF HIS PAST IS AN EXAMPLE TO OTHER MEN WHO STRUGGLE IN THEIR SOULS.**

Ardell is currently the apostle and overseer of Spoken Word Ministries. He is the managing director of Operation Boomerang, an outreach program that ministers to people who have succumbed to adverse lifestyles. He also holds personal deliverance and counseling sessions with key (male) leaders around the world. Ardell has a burden for men to be fathers and husbands who can spiritually cover their families and affect a nation. Using his contractor's license, he has also organized Mechanical of Faith, with a vision for training and equipping men to have job trades in the construction industry. Finally, Ardell directs and oversees A Child of the King Learning Center in Jacksonville, Florida. His motto in life is that Jesus brings total healing—mind, body, and spirit!

Ardell says, "If I could come out of what I came out of, I can help others to come out." Ardell is known as a man's man, and he thanks God for being a husband of one wife. He has totally forgiven his father, and the generational curse of the bastard has been broken off of him. The strength of his deliverance from the poverty, bondage, and perversion of his past is an example to other men who struggle in their souls. He proclaims the liberty of the Lord around the world so that people may know that he has experienced what he preaches, and *it is real!*

Jemal Farrell

Jemal Farrell was born in Jamaica, New York, several years after his family moved to the United States from the West Indies. He grew up in the fast lane on the streets of New York. As a result of economic struggle, he was seduced into a lifestyle of dealing drugs. Jemal acquired sources that gave him access to unimaginable amounts of cocaine and heroin. In the midst of his illegal pursuits, he married Jennell. Together they had five children. Outside of his marriage, Jemal had other female associates with whom he lived double lives of adultery. He financially supported them and even had a child out of wedlock as a result of his infidelity.

Under the guise of false success, Jemal headed three drug shops where he managed a twenty-one-man drug ring. The drug business that Jemal created grossed $25,000 a week. Though Jemal never used drugs, the lifestyle of dealing drugs eventually caught up with him. One day his house was robbed by a group of street thugs while he was out of town on business. His wife was not in the room when one of the children opened the door for the strange men. The men pretended to be maintenance men and entered the house. They gagged, tied up, and put Jennell and the children in a closet as they tore holes in the walls looking for drugs. After such a close call, Jemal decided to turn over a new leaf in life and moved to Jacksonville, Florida. Jemal's family attended a service at Spoken Word Ministries where he decided to sell out to Jesus Christ.

As a result of Jemal's supernatural conversion, most of his family members are saved and serving the Lord today. Jemal testifies that most of his old street associates are strung out on drugs, dead, deported from the country, or doing fifteen to twenty years in prison.

Today, Jemal is proud to have served the Lord faithfully for ten years. He is an ordained minister at Spoken Word Ministries. Jemal has traveled the nations, ministering in countries such as Malaysia, Peru, Singapore, Trinidad, and Barbados. He is gifted in the areas of warfare, intercession, and deliverance (casting out demons). Jemal is the lead counselor at Operation Boomerang, an outreach ministry of Spoken Word Ministries, which assists men in transition from a life of criminality. He is also the coordinator of Kimberly Daniels Ministries International Publications Department, where he manages the production, editing, duplication, packaging, and distribution of ministry materials worldwide. He also manages a dinner club (Club 777) and community bookstore (Spread the Word Publishing) organized under the church.

> **JEMAL'S DREAM IS THAT OTHER MEN WHO ARE BOUND IN THEIR SOULS WILL HEAR HIS TESTIMONY, AND DOORS WILL BE OPENED FOR THE INNER HEALING PROCESS TO BEGIN.**

Jemal's entrepreneurship skills did not die on the streets. He has incorporated his own company, Watchman Management, where he owns, manages, renovates, and sells properties in the Jacksonville area. Jemal is proud to have personally contracted the renovation of a $1.6 million building project that Spoken Word Ministries has recently undertaken. All of his work was given as a seed to the ministry. Jemal is one of the major contributors at his church, and he believes that God has charged him to be a financier for the kingdom. The fruit of the project that Jemal has spearheaded at the church is a five-star learning center that accommodates 186 children, a top-of-the-line dinner club that seats 125 guests, and a community bookstore.

Jemal has repented of his infidelity to his wife and God. He has a strong marriage covenant and is humbled that God has delivered him from the spirit of adultery. He is also thankful that he does not struggle with the residue that comes from playing around with the fire of adultery. Jemal's dream is that other men who are bound in their souls will hear his testimony, and doors will be opened for the inner healing process to begin. Jemal says, "There is no true healing without inner healing. It is the healing that goes to bed with you at night and wakes up with you in the morning. My conscience is healed, and all the money in the world cannot replace that."

MARY SCRUGGS

Mary Scruggs is sixty-six years old. Eleven years ago she was diagnosed with Graves' disease. She was going blind and unable to care for herself any longer. She moved from Richmond, Virginia, to Jacksonville, Florida, to live with her son. He was to be her caretaker because of her physical condition.

Mary had been attending a Spirit-filled church in the local area when she met me at a conference. Mary was living holy and loved the Lord, but she struggled with the fear of the symptoms that she had to deal with on a daily basis. She was forced to have surgery on her eyes, and her eyeballs literally bulged from her sockets. I called Mary to the altar for prayer and said, "I see a demon behind your eyes!" Mary had not told anyone of her condition, but the Holy Ghost had her number that day. I made an appointment for Mary to receive deliverance prayer from my husband, Ardell. After hours of prayer, Mary's eyes no longer bulged from her head. The deliverance prayer lead to a physical healing that opened the doors for Mary to be whole again.

> "WHEN GOD HEALS, HE DOES NOT DO HALF A JOB. I AM WHOLE!
> HE HAS BLESSED EVERY PART OF ME."

Today, eleven years later, Mary has no symptoms. She drives a brand-new car and has purchased her own home where she lives alone. Instead of having a caretaker, Mary takes care of the members at the church. She visits the hospitals, frequently praying for the sick. She faithfully volunteers her time at Spoken Word Ministries where she is ordained as a care-pastor. For the past five years, Mary, known to many as "Mother Scruggs," has also overseen the prayer lines at the church. People from around the world call the church to receive prayer from the woman who once so needed prayer herself.

Mary also supervises the infant department at A Child of the King Learning Center. Mary has traveled around the nation on prayer teams with me. She is the proud mother of two children and three grandchildren. Mary states, "When God heals, He does not do half a job. He gave me a full gospel, and I was able to receive my full healing. I am whole! He has blessed every part of me. Now the joy of the Lord is my strength. This strength gives me the ability to take care of myself. My joy is that I am not incapacitated and a burden on my children. Today I have normal vision. When God healed my eyes, He healed my soul. Physical healing and inner healing walk hand in hand when we allow Jesus to do what He does best. *He is the healer!*"

CONCLUSION

MENTAL DISORDERS FROM
A BIBLICAL PERSPECTIVE

P EOPLE ASK THE same question all the time: Is mental illness demonically induced? Because this question does not have a simple answer, I would like to dedicate the conclusion of this book to the discussion of mental disorders from a biblical perspective. In dealing with mind disorders, we must understand that all of them can be characterized as mental illness. In the dictionary *mental illness* is defined as:

> Any of various conditions of the mind characterized by impairment of an individual's normal cognitive, emotional or behavioral functioning, and caused by social, psychological, biochemical, genetic, or other factors, such as infection or head trauma.[1]

What is missing from this picture? As smart as the writers of dictionaries, encyclopedias, and all other informative materials are, how could they leave out "spiritual influence" on the mind? It is as if man's mind, which is a spirit, has no contact with the spirit realm.

The Bible clearly mentions the "mind of the [Holy] Spirit" and the "mind of the flesh" (Rom. 8:6, AMP). This verse states that the mind of the flesh is "sense and reason without the Holy Spirit." It also relates the mind of the flesh to the spirit of death, which comprises all the miseries that arise from sin. Having the mind of the flesh is directly related to misery. Unfortunately, most of the information that we have in relation to mental illness was created from teaching rooted in the mind of the flesh. Great minds attempt to interpret problems and give solutions of the mind with their senses and leave the Holy Spirit out.

> **GOD DOES NOT TAKE KINDLY TO THE WISDOM OF THIS WORLD COMING UP AGAINST THE TRUTH OF HIS WORD.**

Friend, I pray that as you have read this book your spiritual discerner has been sharpened and put on the front burner, and your intellect put on the back.

> For it is written, I will baffle and render useless and destroy the learning of the learned and the philosophy of the philosophers and the cleverness of the clever and the discernment of the discerning; I will frustrate and nullify [them] and bring [them] to nothing. Where is the wise man (the philosopher)? Where is the scribe (the scholar)? Where is the investigator (the logician, the debater) of this present time and age? Has not God shown up the nonsense and the folly of this world's wisdom?
> —1 Corinthians 1:19–20, AMP

Whew! This makes it clear that God does not take kindly to the wisdom of this world coming up against the truth of His Word. God gave Solomon wisdom, and he was the wisest man ever to exist. Wisdom is good in its place, but when it tries to overrule the wisdom of God, it becomes an abomination. Education, knowledge, and intellect are great under the covering of the Most High God. But many build their kingdoms under these false coverings at the expense of many souls.

Back to the question: Is mental illness demonic? I believe that the way society has dealt with mental illness is more demonic than the illness itself. The higher echelons of this world have decided to attempt to heal the minds of men without including the Maker and Healer of the minds. This is very dangerous, and we have paid a great price because of it. Only God can bring restoration to a mind!

Our sports arenas, elementary schools, college campuses, and professional institutions have been taken over by the diabolic plan of the enemy to medicate the minds of men to separate them from God. This is clearly evident in:

+ Steroid usage (athletes)
+ Mood-altering drugs (school-age children)
+ Medications to cope (college campuses/corporate America)

It is the norm to shoot up or pop a pill as the solution to every situation we face today. Many psychiatrists and psychologists have formed legal drug cartels as they are swift to write prescriptions for everything. The pharmacist becomes the street pusher, and the patient becomes the addict. Medical professionals do the business of medication under the guise of trying to make a living. No one will admit that some of these professionals are no different from the *dope man* on the corner.

There is no difference between these two evils in the eyes of God. People are hurting and need help. They do not need temporary solutions that make men rich. The mental health industry of the world has made billions of dollars off the lives of the innocent, but they will not openly admit that they do not have the solution.

I am not totally against the professional resources of mental health. I believe that these resources have their place, and medicine is often needed to accent the solution. The problem comes when we use medicine as the sole source of the solution. It is even a greater problem when we depend on men who do not know God to bring healing and correction to the minds He created. I thank God for doctors like Dr. Don Colbert, who is rooted and grounded in the Lord. He specializes in alternative medicine. I have witnessed and experienced the blessings of it myself. His source is in God, and his methods work. One young lady who was bound by the medication that she was taking for panic disorder was weaned from the medicine and put on natural herbs. The results were unbelievable.

Dr. Colbert also gives his patients scriptures to meditate on. Everything that we need to heal our minds is in the Word of God. We need people who are educated and anointed to line up the Word of God with what they have been taught professionally to set the captives free. Remember, we are spirits, we possess souls, and we live in bodies. All three realms must be dealt with, and it must start with the spirit realm. And no matter what answer you seek, it will be futile if you leave Jesus out!

> **EVERYTHING THAT WE NEED TO HEAL OUR MINDS IS IN THE WORD OF GOD.**

I pray that the contents of this book have stirred your heart to seek wholeness in every area of your life. More than that, I pray that the urgency of the Lord will permeate your inner being to make a difference in the lives of the people with whom God allows you to be in contact on a daily basis.

NOTES

INTRODUCTION
MOVING FORWARD...INSIDE OUT!

1. Thayer and Smith, "Greek Lexicon Entry for Psuche," *The KJV New Testament Greek Lexicon*, http://bible.crosswalk.com/Lexicons/Greek/grk.cgi?number=5590&version=kjv (accessed January 24, 2008).

2. Spiros Zodhiates, *The Complete Word Study Dictionary: New Testament* (Chattanooga, TN: AMG Publishers, 1992), 1494–1495.

CHAPTER 1
INNER HEALING—MINISTRY TO THE WHOLE MAN

1. International Standard Bible Encyclopaedia, Electronic Database, copyright © 1996 by Biblesoft, s.v. "salvation."

CHAPTER 2
THE ESSENCE OF MAN (PART I)

1. Zodhiates, *The Complete Word Study Dictionary: New Testament*, 703.

2. Suomen Jengi, "Scientists Were Afraid Because They Have Opened the Gates of Hell," *Ammennusastia* [Finland], August 1989, translation appearing in Paw Creek Church of God, *The End Times and Victorious Living*, March/April 1990, viewed at http://www.textfiles.com/bbs/KEELYNET/PARANORM/hell1.asc (accessed January 25, 2008).

3. Courtney Seligman, "The Internal Temperatures and Magnetic Fields of the Planets," http://cseligman.com/text/planets/magnetism.htm (accessed January 25, 2008).

CHAPTER 3
THE ESSENCE OF MAN (PART II)

1. Thayer and Smith, "Greek Lexicon Entry for Gumnos," *The KJV New Testament Greek Lexicon*, http://bible.crosswalk.com/Lexicons/Greek/grk.cgi?search=1131&version=kjv&type=eng (accessed January 25, 2008).

CHAPTER 4
EXPERIENCING THE FULLNESS OF SALVATION

1. John Eckhardt, *Prayers That Rout Demons* (Lake Mary, FL: Charisma House, 2008).

CHAPTER 5
WILL YOU BE MADE WHOLE?

1. Library of Congress, "Family Tragedy," Exhibition: The American Colony in Jerusalem, http://www.loc.gov/exhibits/americancolony/ amcolony-family.html (accessed January 28, 2008). Lyrics to "It Is Well With My Soul" by Horatio G. Spafford. Public domain.

2. Library of Congress, "Continuing Relief Work," Exhibition: The American Colony in Jerusalem, http://www.loc.gov/exhibits/ americancolony/amcolony-relief.html (accessed January 28, 2008).

CHAPTER 9
THE NAMES OF GOD

1. For more information on the Hebrew and Aramaic names of God, as well as in-depth information on *El Nosei*, contact Word Bible College at info@wordbiblecollege.org or visit http:// www.wordbiblecollege.org/ and http://www.wordbiblecollege .org/Word%20Bible%20College%20Curriculum%202007-08.pdf.

CHAPTER 10
THE WORD

1. Kimberly Daniels, *Delivered to Destiny* (Lake Mary, FL: Charisma House, 2005).

CHAPTER 11
DELIVERED FROM EMOTIONAL DAMAGE

1. Kimberly Daniels, *Give It Back!* (Lake Mary, FL: Charisma House, 2007).

CHAPTER 12
ADDRESSING THE ISSUE OF SEXUAL PERVERSION

1. "Just My Imagination Running Away With Me" by Barrett Strong and Norman Whitfield. Print license applied for from Hal Leonard Permissions.

2. ePodunk.com, "Where the Boys Are: Georgia," http://www .epodunk.com/county_data2/mw11.html (accessed January 31, 2008).

3. This information was taken from American Psychiatric Association, *Diagnostic and Statistical Manual of Mental Disorders, Fourth Edition* (Washington: American Psychiatric Association, 2000).

CHAPTER 13
THE PRIDE OF LIFE

1. Zodhiates, *The Complete Word Study Dictionary: New Testament*, 853.

CHAPTER 14
GOD HEALS!

1. You can read more about this in my book *Delivered to Destiny*.

CONCLUSION
MENTAL DISORDERS FROM A BIBLICAL PERSPECTIVE

1. Dictionary.com, *The American Heritage Dictionary of the English Language, Fourth Edition* (Boston, MA: Houghton Mifflin Company, 2004), s.v. "mental illness," http://dictionary.reference.com/browse/ mental illness (accessed: February 01, 2008).

Fighting evil requires a
STRATEGY!

If you have been encouraged and challenged by Kimberly Daniels with *Inside Out,* here is another book, written in the same no-holds-barred style, that we think you will enjoy.

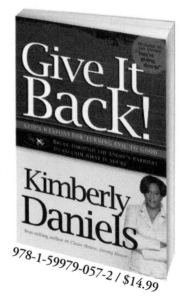

Discover how to recognize Satan's sneaky tactics and use your God-given authority and weapons to put him in his place. Kimberly Daniels teaches powerful principles for spiritual warfare that will prepare and equip you for life's battles.

Visit your local bookstore.

978-1-59979-057-2 / $14.99